More Praise for *The Source of Success*

"What I find so thoroughly refreshing about *The Source of Success* is that it presents a real-world practitioners' approach to challenges which all of us, not just the five hundred men and women who run Fortune 500 firms, face on a day-to-day basis."
　　—Bernard B. Beal, chairman and CEO, M. R. Beal & Company; chairman, A Better Chance

"Peter Georgescu's long career exemplifies integrity and creativity. This profound book demonstrates why those qualities are crucial to success in business today."
　　—Lodewijk de Vink, former chairman, CEO, Warner Lambert

"Peter Georgescu describes the tsunami-like forces sweeping over all companies and industries today, and he provides the keys for survival, success, and prosperity in the new competitive landscape. He walks the walk."
　　—Robert Haas, chairman of the board, Levi Strauss & Co.

"Peter Georgescu writes a winning book, offering great insight and practical guidance to achieving evolutionary leadership through compassion, integrity, and strength of character. No combination is more formidable than strategy and character and the habits of action one develops in meeting great challenges. An invaluable read!"
　　—Steve Heyer, president and CEO, Starwood

"The concept of universal surplus is one every business leader should take to heart. There are few, if any, real sustainable competitive advantages in the business world. As a result, every enterprise has to organize itself to win through intense and sustained change activity at all levels and in all segments of its activities. The five principles are those that can inspire and empower this kind of sustained change in a complex organization. People will follow and multiply the actions of top management in ways we cannot even imagine. Peter brings all this to life in engaging examples."

—Michael H. Jordan, chairman of the board and CEO, EDS

"When Peter Georgescu speaks of the principles essential to success, he means principles, not motivational tools or management gimmicks. *The Source of Success* is fundamentally about developing the character and the wisdom you need to prevail in a highly competitive world. This is an essential book for today's business leaders—and tomorrow's."

—Mike Miles, former chairman, CEO, KFC, Kraft, Philip Morris

"This is a book written by one of America's most innovative and talented business leaders. His notion of a new competitive environment—one where supply greatly exceeds demand—explains why so many once dominant market leaders have faltered. They failed to learn how to compete effectively against faster-moving, more innovative new competitors. But it is Georgescu's firsthand case examples of so many specific leaders' successes and failures where so much learning and wisdom unfold. His experience-based assessment of what it takes to win in today's much more competitive environment alone makes *The Source of Success* worth studying, not just reading."

—Andrall E. Pearson, former chairman, Yum! Brands

"Peter Georgescu's riveting account of his boyhood is, in itself, well worth the price of this book. But his keen insights into the power of creativity and the nature of true leadership are laced with compelling, real-life examples, which make *The Source of Success* a winner, like the author himself."

—Keith Reinhard, chairman, DDB Worldwide

The Source of Success

Peter Georgescu

with David Dorsey

Foreword by Ram Charan

The Source of Success

Five Enduring Principles at the Heart of Real Leadership

JOSSEY-BASS
A Wiley Imprint
www.josseybass.com

Published by Jossey-Bass
A Wiley Imprint
989 Market Street, San Francisco, CA 94103-1741   www.josseybass.com

Jossey-Bass books and products are available through most bookstores. To contact Jossey-Bass directly call our Customer Care Department within the U.S. at 800-956-7739, outside the U.S. at 317-572-3986, or fax 317-572-4002.

Jossey-Bass also publishes its books in a variety of electronic formats. Some content that appears in print may not be available in electronic books.

Library of Congress Cataloging-in-Publication Data
Georgescu, Peter.
  The source of success : five enduring principles at the heart of real leadership / Peter Georgescu, with David Dorsey ; foreword by Ram Charan.–1st ed.
       p. cm.
  Includes index.
  ISBN-13: 978-0-7879-8037-5 (alk. paper)
  ISBN-10: 0-7879-8037-4 (alk. paper)
  1. Leadership. 2. Success. I. Dorsey, David, 1952- II. Title.
  HD57.7.G4586 2005
  658.4'092–dc22   2005010928

Printed in the United States of America
FIRST EDITION
HB Printing   10 9 8 7 6 5 4 3 2 1

Contents

Foreword

This is a book whose time has come. The world of business has changed over the past decade in radical ways, leaving many of us puzzled about how to adapt. We all know how much more competitive the arena is now—or how level the playing field has become—and as a result, many of us look a bit skeptically at some of the old principles for getting ahead. Few of the old truisms about success seem quite equal to the challenge of adapting to all this. As Peter says here, the change we need to make is simple and yet difficult. This is because the world of business has changed in dramatic ways and what it needs now is leadership with character. If you're looking for a quick and easy fix, put this book back on the shelf. This is not a list of ten quick techniques or tactics. It's about fundamental, radical change in the way we think about doing business, and about who we need to be, as people, in order to succeed.

I've been lucky enough to have a close view of how Peter ran Young & Rubicam, working with clients who ranked among the largest companies in the world. We helped them solve core strategic business problems. Peter led his people with honesty, integrity, and a strength and sensitivity that arose from the trials of his childhood in Romania and his education in America. His own leadership was a shining example of the simple principles he lays out in this book. The resulting success at Y&R at every level—in reputation, client satisfaction, new client acquisition, and employee satisfaction—was quite remarkable. The financial results were equally outstanding for the shareholders. *The Source of Success* puts to rest, once and for all, the notion that free enterprise can make a profit at the expense of customers, employees, and the communities where it operates. Free enterprise lives or dies, now, by the relationship, the truth—the loyalty—it creates and sustains. That loyalty springs from the character of those engaged in the enterprise. *The Source of Success* describes the only principles that will work now, but it also shows how these principles, oddly enough, lead to both success *and* personal happiness.

Ultimately, *The Source of Success* equates success in business with the character traits that make for a happy life. The personal and the professional don't diverge anymore: you can't be one person at home and another at work. What makes a person successful is precisely what makes that person whole. Success and happiness work hand in hand, both for organizations and for individuals. Peter calls on everyone to undertake a journey toward a new way of doing business, but it's also a new way of being yourself in your work. The journey will lead in as many different directions as there are people trying to succeed. Where it originates, though, for you, I can say with great confidence: it starts when you turn the page and begin reading this book.

June 2005   RAM CHARAN

Introduction

A friend of mine, who was doing a book on the subject, recently asked me to describe for him the biggest break in my career. It was an interesting question, and a reasonable one. I spent thirty-seven years at Young & Rubicam, retiring as CEO, after helping to establish Y&R as one of the largest advertising and marketing communications agencies in the world. You can't, after all, become the CEO of a major corporation without your share of luck. I've been, perhaps, luckier than many of my counterparts. But my biggest break? That came before I was ever a businessman, or even an American citizen. My success was made possible by lessons I learned fifty years ago, as a young boy in Europe.

I was born and grew up in Romania. Before the Second World War, my father had been a general manager for Standard Oil (now Exxon) in Romania's Ploesti oil fields, the richest oil reservoir in Europe. When the Germans invaded, they arrested and imprisoned him as an enemy. My parents were brave people. During his stay in prison, my father, with the help of many patriotic Romanians and the Allied forces through the OSS, planned and executed a coup against the Germans. As a result, when the Russians came through that country in early 1945, the Germans hardly put up a fight. But our Communist rulers turned out to be as bad as the Nazis.

When I was eight years old, two years after the end of the war, my father was free again and went to work for the oil company. In the early winter of 1947, my parents took a scheduled trip to Exxon's headquarters in New York. When it was time to return, they weren't allowed back into Romania. The iron curtain had fallen around the new Soviet empire, including our homeland. The

Communist putsch took hold, and now my parents were labeled dirty bourgeois imperialists and evil capitalists. Had he returned, my father—once again considered an enemy of the state—would have found himself back in prison, or worse.

Dazed by all the turmoil, my brother, Costa, and I retreated to Lipova, a small town in Transylvania, to live with my grandparents in their country villa, where we thought we would be safe. Their mansion was a national treasure. It housed my grandfather's 70,000-book library and my grandmother's rooms full of Romanian peasant costumes, beautifully embroidered. My grandfather—my mother's father—had been a successful politician, the governor of Banat, the largest region of Romania's west. In the *new* Romania, he was considered a potential insurgent—like my father.

Early one morning we found our two shepherd dogs dead in the garden, poisoned. We had no idea who had done it, or why. We went to bed that night, in mourning for them, and then, just before daybreak, awoke to the sound of boots on our marble floors. How I came to despise boots, German boots, Russian boots, and now Romanian ones. The Communists had burst into our home to arrest my grandfather, then seventy-nine years old. (We later learned that he was one of hundreds of thousands arrested— Romania's intelligentsia, generations of politicians and other would-be leaders—all to be exterminated, put to work in open fields, underfed and underclothed, or just locked up in century-old dungeons until they withered away and died.) I'll never forget the serene face of my old grandpa, trying to console us, though he knew he would never see us again. That terrible morning, I saw what evil can do, rising up in the most ordinary, otherwise benevolent hearts.

My brother and I were taken from our new home in Lipova, along with our grandmother, and transported across the country to Botosian, a town close to the Russian border in Eastern Romania. We were given a series of humiliating, dangerous jobs, leaving for work at 6 A.M. and returning home twelve hours later, six days a week. I had to do the vilest tasks. I went into the sewers to clear out sand and excrement. I was promoted to work for the local electric company, but I inherited the nightmare job no one else wanted: getting up around four o'clock each morning to walk around in the dark, shutting down transformers that meted out Botosian's electrical usage. The transformers were housed in tall metal cabinets, located on various street corners, and when my hand bumped into the wrong piece of metal, a searing jolt knocked me out cold.

One year stretched into the next, and we received only occasional letters from our parents—which were smuggled in. In the final years, we heard nothing. I defended myself against dread and despair by becoming a stubborn, defiant worker: adapting to a work-camp meritocracy that existed only in my imagination. I forced myself to believe that if I worked hard enough and well enough, I would be recognized, promoted, slowly earning the respect of my captors, maybe even my freedom. It was a fantasy, but, as a result, I became a hard worker.

Then, one day in March 1954—six years after we were taken captive—Costa and I and our grandmother were told to pack up what little we had. It was time to leave. We had no idea whether we were heading toward freedom or deeper into captivity. Escorted by the usual phalanx of guards, we were taken to catch the overnight train to Bucharest. We arrived in the Romanian capital the next morning, where our uncle, Ionel Manolescu, met us at the train station. The surprise of seeing his unexpected face was a moment of supreme joy. He was one of the most famous members of our family, a well-known stage and movie actor. His smile was, for us, the face of freedom itself.

It was true. We were going to be reunited with our parents in America. For two or three weeks, we stayed with our uncle in his posh Bucharest apartment, waiting for our passports. We took luxurious baths with endless hot water, slept in feather beds, ate all we wanted. Finally, early in April, Costa and I, giddy with excitement, made our way to the train station, where we exchanged tearful farewells with our grandmother, who would stay behind. We boarded the overnight train for Vienna. On the way, we learned what seemed quite miraculous: the government of the United States had interceded to free us.

In the morning, we arrived in Vienna. Our father met us on the platform. There was an instant of shock—we'd grown so much—but it was swept aside in a wave of excitement, tenderness, and pleasure as we rushed into one another's arms. The next day, we flew to America, to New York's Idlewild Airport—now JFK. The spires of Manhattan were breathtaking, breaking through the clouds as we descended. On the ground, we met our mother in a tearful, joyous reunion, with dozens of cameras flashing around us. We were famous. But how? Why?

Like countless refugees before me, I began life anew in America. Our rescue made everything possible. But the part that means the most to me now is the way the rescue happened. Our father told us how Romanian agents had approached my parents in the United States and asked my father to spy for the Communists in exchange for our safety. Being an influential executive, my father would have been in a position to do that. After a night of agonized reflection, with great trepidation, my father and mother decided to call the FBI, which sent two agents to their home. They were told they had two choices: one was to play along with the offer, pretend to spy for the Communists, while American intelligence would actually be using them as double agents, feeding false information to the Romanians. Neither of them felt comfortable becoming involved in the dubious ethics of a game like that. The second option, the one they chose, was to take their story to the press. The idea was to create a scandal of such magnitude that the Romanians and Russians would be forced to protect us. It was dangerous: they had no way to know what it would provoke our captors to do. It was the right thing to do, the ethical thing, but far riskier than collaboration with the enemy.

With the help of a public relations expert at the FBI, the news of our story—the espionage gambit, the way the Communists were holding us hostage—reached millions of ears around the globe.

Newspapers and magazines, including *Time, Newsweek, Life,* and the *Saturday Evening Post,* wrote stories about us, and television news, then in its infancy, covered the story as well. It provoked an outpouring of sympathy around the world.

Outraged by our plight—and by Romania's craven attempt to use two innocent children as leverage for espionage—Frances Payne Bolton, a ranking Republican on the House Foreign Relations Committee, buttonholed the Soviet foreign minister, Andrei Vyshinsky, in an elevator after a U.N. meeting in 1953 and demanded our release. She and my parents continued to work behind the scenes, pushing for help. As a result, Eisenhower asked the Romanian Prime Minister Gheorghe Gheorghiu-Dej to set us free. Still, nothing happened. Finally, secretly, the United States traded a Soviet spy in exchange for the Georgescu boys. None of this came out, but it was the story told around our home.

The breaks to follow weren't nearly as magical as my liberation from Romania, but there were many—all of them, in one way or another, smaller reverberations of the first. I was accepted into Exeter Academy. That was a gift. Then I earned my way into Princeton, and finally Stanford Business School. And I was offered a job at Y&R right out of Stanford, and stayed there for my entire career.

My big break wasn't a matter of luck. It was in having parents with the courage and integrity to do the right thing. They spent one harrowing night debating whether they should spy on the American government to save the lives of their children, and chose, instead, to go to the world with the truth. It might have resulted in a swift death for Costa and me, and maybe my grandmother. They had no way of knowing. But to them it was the only genuine alternative to a life of shame. Their leap of faith wasn't just the right thing to do: it *worked*. Their integrity, their courage, and their honesty—in short, their example—became core values for my life, values I tried to instill at Y&R. They were the values, ultimately, that enabled me to succeed.

This book is about a world utterly removed from the one in which I grew up. It's a world so different that it couldn't have been imagined a couple of decades ago. Many of our fundamental assumptions about how the world works have been shaken. In such a world you would think the values I learned as a child would be hopelessly outdated, but there's a paradox at the heart of where we find ourselves now. These values—honesty, integrity, truth, accountability have become *more* important and relevant than ever. Indeed, they're essential to success in a way that hasn't been the case for quite a long while, if ever. This new world of business asks you, and indeed enables you, to remain faithful to the most fundamental dimensions of your humanity.

I've come to these conclusions because, for more than thirty years, I've seen firsthand how the world is changing and how things get done at the top—both right and wrong—partly because I was there at the top, *trying* to get things done the right way. My career gave me a rare passkey into the highest offices of some of the world's largest corporations. Y&R was a global advertising agency with 460 offices throughout 82 countries. I worked closely with those who led many of the giants: Danone, Ford, AT&T, Sony, IBM, Colgate, Johnson & Johnson, KFC, Kodak, Metropolitan Life, Sears, and the U.S. Army, to name a few.

During my tenure, my team and I took our company public during a period that saw our revenues increase threefold—while profits grew to nine times their size when I began. In that period, the company became more than an ad agency: we worked as partners with the CEOs and officers of the world's largest and most prominent corporations. In our role as consultants, we helped some of these companies shape their entire strategic vision.

I've seen the world evolve and come to understand that the values and principles in this book are the only ones that will work, from now on. We are at the end of one world and the beginning of another. The world in the last decade has changed—in many ways, it seems, for the worse—and yet there has never been a time for greater hope and confidence. We can unleash a tremendous, untapped reservoir of energy within ourselves and our organizations if we understand the nature of the new economic world we face and the business model it requires.

This book outlines the nature of this changed world and charts a new strategic model and a source of success in a world that no longer responds to mere tactics. Everything in our future depends on a shift that shakes some of our deepest assumptions about what it takes to succeed. There *is* a new economy, but it isn't quite the one everyone celebrated in such a facile way a few years ago.

The Source of Success will show you how to adapt to this fundamental and unprecedented shift by following five enduring principles. Behind all these principles is the oldest lesson of all—it pays to be honest and decent—an old lesson with a peculiarly new relevance to the world of business. I believe we can maintain the moral compass of daily life and make it the heart of the way we do business. Business must reinvent the way it operates. We, as individuals, must reinvent the way we think, the way we act, and the way we treat others and ourselves. We must adapt to how the *world* is changing—in a way that's honest and accountable to customers, employees, and shareholders—in order to expand and enhance our standard of living and the quality of our lives. A new business paradigm has emerged for this economy, which I'm about to describe in the first chapter of this book.

To understand how all of this is not only possible but urgently necessary, it is imperative to comprehend the major forces shaping our destiny. These forces are the consequence of the economic revolution that began a decade ago, and they will continue to drive the course of history for years to come.

June 2005
New York City

Peter Georgescu

To Baggy

The Source of Success

1

THE END OF THE WORLD
AS WE KNOW IT

Many have the will to win. Few have the will
to prepare.

—*Anonymous*

Imagine a business executive in his late fifties, wearing pinstripes, standing before an audience of similar business types and playing a recording of R.E.M.'s "The End of the World as We Know It." Imagine an audience, hoping to hear a subtle analysis of business and the economy but getting an earful of Michael Stipe's voice instead of their featured speaker's—and not quite knowing what to make of it. Well, I was the DJ in the tailored suit, at least for the length of that song, and I was playing it for an assembly of top management and telecommunications experts at AT&T's training center in New Jersey because it seemed to me, at the time, the perfect anthem for what was happening in the world of business.

AT&T was in the middle of a cultural shift. A new CEO had arrived, bringing a new team with him. That period of flux forced me to reflect critically about AT&T's aggressive strategy of promoting itself as the lowest-cost provider of telephone services. Its marketing centered on promotion and low price. It was all about packages, friend deals, family deals—price price price. And it all struck me as a terrible kind of dead end. Keep heading down that path and there would be no way back for the company.

So I was going into the meeting with a sense of deep concern about AT&T's future, and my concern wasn't about how AT&T would come up with a new ad campaign. My words would be about matters of life and death for the corporation. My concern was about the corporation's deepest mission, of how it was going to build new relationships with customers on the foundation of a new approach to its role in the lives of those customers. It was my job, standing before those executives, to tell them they would go out of business if they kept selling on the basis of price. It was a make-or-break situation for both AT&T and Y&R: we wanted and needed their business. But they had to hear the hard truth.

It occurred to me as I finalized my speech the night before that, as CEO of Young & Rubicam in the late 1990s, I'd begun to face the same problems. We were all in the same boat. Good advertising, good PR, good communications of any sort, seemed easier to get than ever before, at lower and lower prices. How could this be? Why was this happening to all of us? We were experts—in all these camps—with a rare set of skills. Our talents were generating premium services and products that, it seemed, might eventually be sold for bargain-basement prices. It didn't make sense.

That night, though—the night just before I was to give my speech—the way back from this dead end suddenly became apparent to me. I realized what was happening in the world of business and how to respond to it. So I went into that meeting, not with a sense of foreboding, but with a genuine sense of delight: I told them the world they knew had ended, but I offered this to them as good news. Something much better was about to take its place. We were all about to recognize a new source of success. And I explained what it was. As a result, AT&T pulled back from a disastrous course and reshaped its vision of its role in people's lives. The CEO and his team listened, and the brilliant chief brand officer, Marilyn Laurie, worked with us on an inspirational marketing campaign. We created advertising about how AT&T was helping people connect with one another, images of mothers working on the beach, tele-conferencing while their children played in the sand. Powerful advertising to the sounds of "Amazing Grace" and Elton John's "Rocket Man." And yet the advertising itself wouldn't have worked if AT&T hadn't reshaped its strategic vision: its sense of its own role in the lives of its customers. For two years, the company rebounded and differentiated itself. Unfortunately, when manage-ment decided to expand through acquisitions outside the core and deemphasize the traditional consumer business, they lost their way. Early in 2005, old Ma Bell got bought.

Too Much of a Good Thing

I told those executives the world has crossed an unprecedented threshold: too much of a good thing has become a permanent way of life. For the first time in history, the supply of almost everything has begun to exceed demand, *in a way that isn't cyclical*. This isn't temporary. We can't wait it out. We must change the way we do business to adapt to a lasting new economic landscape. In other words, we will likely never again see a world of scarcity for any length of time. We've entered a world of permanent excess supply. Almost everyone now acknowledges a cyclical downturn where supply will exceed demand for quite a while, but few see this condition as permanent. It isn't simply the result of an economic recession—surpluses are here to stay. As a result, everything is becoming a commodity. Everything.

An old world has ended, and a new one has begun. This isn't happening to the telecommunications industry alone. It's happen-ing to everyone in the developed world—or soon will. Partly as a result of the ascendancy of free enterprise, productivity will now outstrip demand for years and decades, perhaps forever. We now have the means, the technology, to make more of what people want and with ever lower costs. As a result, people may choose to buy from you, but they don't have to. They can buy from someone else just as easily. We have crossed a revolutionary threshold in world history, with overcapacity everywhere bumping up against diminishing demand in the developed world. This shift has enormous economic, social, and even political implications.

The reason many of us haven't recognized the permanent reality of excess supply is this: it didn't happen overnight, all at once. It sneaked onto the scene, thieving its way through one industry after another. Why the shift? You might be tempted to think technology alone has driven it. But it isn't that simple.

An entire network of complex factors has converged, so that everything that used to serve as a choke point to protect market domination has fallen away. With knowledge, expertise, technology, capital, labor, raw materials, and manufacturing capacity so readily available, most barriers to entry into any industry have broken down. Cash is cheap and easy to get. The tolerance for debt, on all levels of our economy, is now immense, and though this may not be a good thing in itself, it has ensured growth, competition, and the quick translation of good ideas into profitable businesses.

In the old postwar world (from 1950 through 1990), where demand for goods, services, capital, talent, and distribution capacity generally outran supply, most industries could make a profit with relative ease. Because the marketplace wanted more goods and services than business could deliver—and because the financial, technological, geographical, and regulatory barriers to competition were relatively high—businesses, prices, and economies could generally grow at a predictable and healthy pace. Build a new factory or open a new office and it was likely that everything you could produce there would be bought by the world's emerging middle classes.

This is no longer true. With little fanfare, the 1990s witnessed a change to a world of excess supply on almost every front. Money is no longer scarce; it's now relatively easy for any business or businessperson to finance an enterprise built around a smart idea. Skilled labor is plentiful. Although there may be local labor shortages in particular skills, talent is abundant on a global level. (Computer programmers are found in Bombay, San Antonio, Kuala Lumpur, and even Bucharest—all reachable via the Internet.) Distribution channels? Selling and shipping extend around the globe overnight now, thanks to the Internet. Few companies have major difficulties in bringing their products or services to the marketplace. Information and ideas travel freely. And innovation and invention rarely shield any company from competition for more than several months—or, in some cases, even a few days.

You might object that the supply of oil, say, or of Moet & Chandon champagne is limited and will always be, therefore, expensive. But the limitations on our supply of both are largely artificial. Those resources, if you consider wine a valuable natural resource— as I do—are actually quite plentiful. Those who control the supply of oil have limited the world's access to that supply to boost prices to artificially high levels. And Moet & Chandon has, in reality, millions of bottles of its elixir stored away. Copper, iron, magnesium, zinc: won't those resources run out? Possibly, down the road, but with most of them, science and technology will come up with ample supplies of artificial substitutes. PVC pipes are a perfectly suitable replacement for copper ones. And our technological ingenuity has already come up with a variety of alternative fuel technologies to eliminate our dependency on fossil fuel, if we choose to adapt our habits, and our industries, to take advantage of them.

As a result, throughout the developed world, there is—or will be—a significant oversupply of most goods and services. I'm not just referring to the dozen different labels of bottled water on grocery shelves, or the almost interchangeable brands of personal computers on sale as commodities at ever-lower prices. The fact is that overcapacity is huge in virtually every line of business. Auto factories already in operation can produce 30 percent more cars per year than people actually need. As a result, we have too many cars, computers, networks of dark fiber-optic cable already in the ground: all the outcome of overcapacity everywhere.

This paradigm shift is, in many ways, a wonderful event. It means that the struggle between consumers and providers—which extends back to before recorded history and the bazaars of Mesopotamia—has been decided. The consumers have won. In the world of excess supply, consumers are the real leaders of business now. They are in a position to call the shots based on what they want—not on what manufacturers, marketers, distributors, advertisers, or retailers are willing to make and sell.

This shift has disturbing implications for business. In the new world, what was once friendly competition for market share in a comfortable, clubby atmosphere where there were plenty of buyers to go around has become a battle where every company's survival is always at stake. And competition is likely to become even more intense in the years ahead.

At the same time, many competing products and services have become impossible to tell apart. Worthwhile innovations are rapidly imitated; today's unique benefit is tomorrow's standard feature. What would have ensured years of profit in the past is now a mere ticket into the competitive arena. Products that once stood alone now face dozens, sometimes hundreds of competitors. Once-powerful brands are converging into commodities differentiated—if at all—by price alone. Multiple brands are perceived to have equal value. And in this price-sensitive, hotly competitive world, profit margins are under constant downward pressure. Commoditization is the cancer of twenty-first century business.

It's a brutal business environment. Some of the old tactical responses to a downturn in demand will still work, up to a point. Companies continue to cut costs, but there's a limit to how much they can cut without impairing quality. Companies may increase productivity per worker, but productivity gains are up against the law of diminishing returns. Ironically, this environment is forcing us to reinvent how we make and sell products and services in a way that, over the long run, will usher in a far more personal, humane style of doing business. Long-term success is requiring business leaders to compete according to a set of rules and values quite different from those that brought prosperity down through history.

The Internet is playing a key role in this shift. It's a truly revolutionary force, one with the manifest potential to obliterate borders and strengthen even further the consumer's control over business. It amplifies every individual's voice as a buyer and—at least as important—as a citizen. It's also global, the first and (so far) only truly worldwide communications medium in history. It's available to anyone with access to a computer at a fraction of the cost of any other medium.

The Internet amplifies what the economy is already doing: it empowers individuals as buyers—to shop for the best price from dealers or suppliers around the world in a matter of seconds. It also lets businesses shape processes and practices from the ground up. In the past, gathering, analyzing, communicating, and sharing information was difficult and costly. The Internet makes it far easier and cheaper to start and run a business. It allows a company to leapfrog or streamline most traditional supply, production, distribution, and sales channels. It makes world-class customer service more readily available than ever.

The Internet makes it possible to eliminate from our business processes virtually anything that does not add value. This intensifies competition: start-ups with a great idea and a good business model catch up with veterans in a matter of months. All this drives down prices and creates pressure to improve products and services. Nothing holds its value for long. When things are so easy to get, prices, margins, and profits fall and keep falling.

What's needed is a new business model that encourages constant innovation while drastically eliminating intermediate steps between the customer and the producer of a product or service. A new business model must stimulate demand by creating friendships with individual customers, a personalized way of doing business that builds a brand identity, an intimacy of service, that customers trust above all others.

Freedom Has Won

No one, down through history, predicted the revolution we're going through right now. Over the past several decades, communism collapsed and freedom won. Communism died out of sheer exhaustion. It destroyed the economic energy and inventiveness only freedom generates. But something entirely unexpected happened, as well: capitalism has waned, too.

To say capitalism is withering may sound a bit premature to people who still live in a free society and work in a free market. Yet freedom, not capital, is what generates economic growth now. The distinction between these two is more than semantics, though the transformation of capitalism is a reality that still isn't universally acknowledged. By capitalism, I mean the way wealth and resources it could buy—scarce for most, plentiful for the powerful few—can control the conditions by which people work and live. Concentrations of capital were once used to control opportunity for those without access to them. Such concentrations of resources no longer distinguish between success and failure: hoarding is no longer a reliable way to protect and increase power. Conventional wisdom credits capitalism as the force that creates value in the modern business world. America is still identified as the most powerful capitalistic empire in the history of the world. Capitalism, after all, defeated communism in the long cold war against the Soviet Union. More recently, it has been cast as the villain by those in the developing world, looking for a scapegoat to blame for the fragile, half-starving economic conditions in many Middle Eastern and African economies.

Even so, capitalism *is* declining, and free enterprise is only getting stronger. Look at where the most explosive economic growth is happening now: China. The engine of growth in that socialist and still authoritarian nation isn't capitalism: it's free enterprise. The Chinese government, to compete successfully with the rest of the world, saw the need to lift its heavy-handed control through a centralized economy and move aggressively toward free enterprise. In India, the same is true. In this century, free enterprise will be the mainstay of growth and economic success. And by free enterprise, I mean the ability of economic forces to operate efficiently and effectively in *relative* freedom, producing products and services, and thus wealth. This sort of freedom is a proven concept. At the high points in our recent economic history—for ideas that inspired the confidence of investors—readily available capital and other resources have fueled the capacity of business to create value, inspiring innovations and ultimately producing growth. Those resources didn't convey power or value: easy access to them is what made it possible for entrepreneurial creativity to grow. The power came from inventiveness supported by affordable access to resources, capital, and labor. Inevitably, free enterprise, if it takes hold, will drive toward ever-greater political freedom.

This unhindered creativity—the heart of free enterprise—fosters competition while continuously improving quality and reducing prices to consumers and customers. Capitalism as a force in economic and political power has withered because today capital is far more widely available—and relatively cheap. It is still an important commodity, and access to global capital markets remains essential to business success. But access to resources no longer determines the standard of living of nations or the business success of companies. The easiest way to fulfill desires and needs, to get things done, is through the convergence of ideas, resources, and capital in a free market—in other words, through free enterprise. But the power now resides in the creative idea, not the money that allows it to become a reality.

In the relatively modern economic era—the past two hundred years—wealth-producing growth has developed in cycles around five technologically driven economic revolutions. Carlota Perez, a brilliant Venezuelan-born economist and general social scientist, has created a predictable model for how these technological revolutions have come to pass, the needed ingredients to produce the actual revolutions, and the costs, both economic and social, associated with these revolutions. In her own words:

> For each technological revolution, that time-lag is characterized by strong divergence in the rates of growth of industries, countries and regions . . . [bringing] the greatest excitement in financial markets, where brilliant successes and innovations share the stage with great manias and outrageous swindles. [These periods] have also ended with the most virulent crashes, recessions and depressions, later to give way, through the establishment of appropriate institutions, to a period of widespread prosperity, based on the potential of that particular set of technologies.

The critical insight is that these wealth-producing revolutions, these advances in technology, have occurred in nations with the most unfettered economies and with the greatest entrepreneurial cultures. Technological revolutions are dramatically creative. And the implementation of new technological paradigms requires courage, risk taking, and entrepreneurial spirit, along with the availability of financial capital and other resources.

Free enterprise is the natural home for new economic world orders and the abundance it generates. No such innovations have ever occurred in controlled economies dominated by communists or heavy-handed socialist ideologies.

In today's world, China and India are progressing at unimaginable rates because they are beginning to embrace free enterprise. Over the past two decades some half a billion people in China and India have been removed from the shackles of poverty into middle-class status thanks to the miraculous power of free enterprise. On the other side, the billion-plus Muslim world by and large languishes in stagnation and hopelessness, disconnected from the global free enterprise wealth-creating engine, and deprived of basic infrastructure and education—a situation that should be a major area of concern for all the people in the developed world.

It is important to note that the markets of the world are not totally free from interference today—nor should they be. Governments and other political forces still temper the creative ferment of free markets. Some of this interference is highly warranted, some not. Most of the time, protectionism is the best example of misguided interference. I would argue that protectionism has been consistently associated with failure, unfairness, increasing poverty, and lack of sustained success. Protectionism has seldom helped weak nations or weak industries get strong. It's simply bad medicine.

The oligopolistic powers of the oil-producing nations are another example. By artificially reducing oil supply, these nations aim to keep oil prices artificially high—harking back to capitalism's traditional chokehold on resources. But they will do this for a limited time and to their eventual detriment. The developed world will unleash new energy strategies designed to end dependence on fossil fuel. Hydrogen, nuclear power, solar power, among other existing or new technologies propelled by private and government investment, will produce economically sound, environmentally cleaner alternatives. Conservation will also play a role to bridge the gap between the two energy eras. And long before that new energy prospect becomes reality, oil prices will drop dramatically as the oil nations race to cash in before the inevitable end of fossil fuel becomes a fact. History has proven this pattern in every other scarce resource cycle. Oil will be no exception.

Clearly, free enterprise needs some referees to officiate the game. Very much like freedom for individuals, where "responsible freedom" is the only practical concept, at this stage of our human development, free enterprise will work only in a world where the rules of the game are clear, transparent, enforceable, and ensure a level playing field for all contenders.

Free media, cross-national watchdog institutions, and governments must play the officiating role in free market competition. This is an essential and positive activity, as it is in athletics. In any team sport, the referee is not an active player, but without a referee, most games would turn ugly. The rules must be clear and aggressively enforced. Our recent history of corporate financial crimes has illustrated this in an inescapable way. When CEOs engineer their balance sheets to pilfer millions of dollars for their own personal use, and when top executives get rich in companies like Enron or WorldCom where average employees and shareholders have lost their life savings or a large portion of their investment, the system breaks down. As a result of crimes at a variety of companies—MCI, WorldCom, Tyco, Enron, Adelphia, Arthur Anderson, Global Crossing, Qwest Communications International, and others—a widespread loss of trust in the way the entire free market operates has become a factor in the stagnation of the current economy.

Governments have another key role to play in a free enterprise economy in addition to being the guardians of fair behavior, enforcers of evolving rules of business engagement, and preservers of public trust among the investing public. Governments must also protect and enhance the "common good" in societies.

Before free enterprise can operate effectively, basic market conditions must exist that enable free enterprise to function. Education is a critical example. Without an educated workforce, free enterprise cannot perform its magic, or even exist. This is one of the major challenges for developing nations—the Arab world in particular and much of Africa. By contrast, it is one of the vital enablers for much of India's and China's ability to propel their economies into the modern world. And for the U.S. economy, a well-educated workforce with the latest state-of-the-art competencies will be one of the fundamental foundations for our continuing success.

A second example of positive government support of free enterprise is the building and maintaining of common-good infrastructure in nations and societies. Simple basics—roads, supplies of clean water, airports, communication links among local communities and with world markets—are also essential. Over time, private enterprise may displace some of these governmental functions, but in the early stages, government support of the common good is an essential element for free enterprise to exist and thrive. The last example of positive government support of free enterprise are strategic investments in common-good causes where the cost is too large for free market investment by private capital, and the time frame required for adequate return is judged too long. The Genome project is a case in point. As private enterprise explored the business opportunities in this area, the advancement of the basic science needed to unearth the complex makeup of our human genes was judged by society as a worthy common-good investment—by the U.S. government. Critically important, all the knowledge discovered in the public sector was immediately made available to the world. Private enterprise—the free enterprise process—took over to apply the discoveries efficiently by developing life-enhancing drugs and clinical treatments.

Both the governments of the world and all private enterprises have an implicit contract with the earth and its environment. We have been given temporary custody, to care for it, to act responsibly toward it, and to respect it. Our actions to date must be modified. We must leave behind for our children and the millennia to come a place better than the one we found. This must be taken to heart and each of us must take on more personal responsibility to advance this imperative cause.

Finally, governments have an important role to play in softening the social impact of the technological revolutions that occur on a forty- to fifty-year cycle. As new technologies displace old institutions, social disruption follows. Jobs are displaced, eliminated. Support systems developed by previous institutions can collapse. Governments, NGOs, world trade organizations have a constructive role to play in protecting the common good, providing a softer landing for the outgoing technological paradigm and helping to usher in the new economic order. By understanding the relatively predictable pattern of these dramatic changes, governments can anticipate societal needs and help embrace change constructively at a lower human cost. Alan Greenspan's management of monetary policy is one such example. Over time, governments can do much more through such things as adult education, retraining, and a faster response to changing economic conditions.

But when it's all said and done, free enterprise is the only wealth-producing engine for the free world. It is in fact business and free enterprise that produce our standard of living. Only business, through free enterprise, can continue to provide the means for our children and our children's children to enjoy the benefits of rich and fulfilling lives. With the help of governments, new social and business institutions will be built, greater fairness, transparency, and level playing fields will become reality, and free enterprise will usher in new epochs of wealth. The unique marriage of creative technological innovations and free enterprise can sustain a rising standard of living for all people on earth. As we look to the future, global free enterprise will grow, change, adapt, and thrive. It will continue to be *the* force for value creation.

We Must Connect with the Disconnected

The profound yet quiet revolutions we've been discussing are colliding with another force for change, adding an immense layer of anxiety for anyone who does business in the global economy. Along with the triumph of free enterprise and the advent of excess supply, global instability is changing the character of business in this century, instilling fear and insecurity in every heart.

While the developed world may soon experience an excess supply of everything it needs, for all too many people on the planet, that surplus has no impact. While the developed nations luxuriate in a glut of fiber-optic cable, much of the Third World is in dire need of corn and flour and clean water. The radical disconnect between these worlds is both immense and perilous. The problem isn't how to produce a few more cars or computers—the problem is getting enough buying power into the hands of people who, at this point, hardly need any product other than a meal. Urging companies or nations to give away their surpluses simply doesn't work. We can argue about how much aid should be sent to the impoverished nations—a great deal more, in my own view. But in the end the only lasting solution to poverty lies with connecting the disconnected and showing them how to increase the value of what they do so that—the selfish dimension of this imperative will be obvious—entrepreneurs can discover ways of *selling* these people the things they need.

Business has become the most powerful force for change in the world. Today, questions of global political and economic significance are not being decided solely by national governments but also by competition among businesses operating in a worldwide market. Therefore, business leadership needs to take into account economic and political realities around the globe. Business leadership needs to acknowledge its responsibility to the people of the world.

Billions of youths are growing up in poverty and deprivation and ignorance in the Middle East, Africa, and parts of Asia. Among them are the potential warriors and terrorists of tomorrow, the future supporters of misguided movements who consider themselves victims, and who blame us in the West as their oppressors. As these nations—and these youths—get poorer and poorer, conditions in those countries become more and more volatile and hostile.

Often the only education these young people get is at the hands of false prophets—fanatics, under the guise of religion, who are only too eager to warp young minds with a sense of hopelessness, a sense of being victimized by the Western world that, they say, deprives them of the quality of life they would have had without our interference. Worse yet, they claim, we in the West want to rob them of their values, their religion, their culture. We don't. But we *do* need to intervene—these youths can no longer be ignored.

These conditions represent an unpredictable force for change. With all the world's economies so intimately linked now, when one part of the web twitches, the entire structure trembles. These problems are far beyond the ability of one business, or even any one coalition of businesses, to solve. But individual companies must choose to act in a way that moves toward a solution to these problems. If you choose to behave as if your behavior were to be replicated by thousands of others, chances are, it will. The comforting isolation of an earlier time no longer works. What the uneducated young think of us matters, because they can do us great harm. The catastrophic attack on the World Trade Center, the tragic train attack in Spain, the endless killings by suicide bombers in Israel and Iraq, all make clear the urgency of this mission—the disconnected of the world will quickly become the enemy of free enterprise if free enterprise offers them no hope.

Military force may well be essential from time to time. But military coercion will never by itself provide a lasting solution. Ultimately, it will require the coming together of individuals, the leading nations of the developed world, the United Nations, the local governments and regional alliances in the developing areas of the world, and successful businesses—all working in harmony—to connect the hopeless and dispirited with the value-creating force of free enterprise.

It will take collaborative effort of the qualified and the willing to start with basic education, the learning of craft, the building of infrastructures, of incentive to businesses to build factories and produce goods in the populated, underdeveloped areas—all for the common good of all people on earth.

Meanwhile, we'd better get used to living and working in an atmosphere of continuous anxiety, insecurity, and risk, until the leaders of the world develop a sufficiently urgent vision to address this critical problem for the benefit of all.

A New Model for the Developed World

Given all these forces, the only question that matters is this: *Is there any predictable way to succeed for long in this environment?* In the shift from excess demand to excess supply, a new model has emerged, turning the old ways of doing things upside down while structuring all business activity around the two remaining sources of value: the customer and the creative employee. Understanding how to build your business around these two is the new source of success. What I have to say about this in the following pages may be tough to accept, at first. Adaptation, giving up the sort of behavior that has kept us alive down through history, making choices based on principle rather than expedience, requires long-term thinking as well as a fundamental change of character in the way we treat those who work for us and buy from us.

The ability to delay gratification and initiate changes that take time to yield results has never come easily for business leaders. In business, we go after profits the way a dog goes after a bone: we structure our organizations so that we're rewarded for immediate results. We want everything, and we want it this quarter. Wall Street has taught us that neither genuine strategic planning nor deep understanding of a changing new economic order are seriously valued.

To sustain success now, you must be able to do both: provide annual profits without fail by developing the vision, culture, and critical imperatives that inspire customer and workforce loyalty. The principles that illuminate the way are creativity, enlightened leadership, competency, alignment, and values. The payoff is precisely in the path itself: adhering to the vision of this book will make your journey an end in itself. This can't be based on the tactics and techniques of the day but on bedrock understanding of the world and the critical underpinnings of a successful enterprise. You still have to bring the will to succeed—but this book can show you the way.

When I stood in front of those AT&T executives, I was optimistic. Yes, I did play my song for them: "It's the end of the world as we know it." But as the song's refrain goes on to say: "and I feel fine." I felt fine then, and I still do, and so should you, if you master and follow the five fundamental principles: creativity, enlightened leadership, competency, alignment, and values. These principles need to be understood, challenged, and eventually accepted. More than that, they will become a source of delight and inner peace once they begin to work. When confronted by the challenges of everyday business life, big and small, it's a wonderful thing to be able to respond instinctively the right way—not simply because it's right, but knowing the time has come when doing the good thing is precisely what will bring success now.

2

CREATIVITY

Tomorrow's Factory Today

The advertising business, more than a century old now, is an industry that doesn't simply rely on creativity: it *sells* creativity. And it does so in a way that is remarkable: by embodying a creative idea in a few images and words, sometimes in nothing more than a corporate logo. There is no better place to see and study the magical power of creative insight in business than through this industry.

In 1953, Miller Brewing Co. was a tiny enterprise out of Milwaukee. Marketing research, courage, risk-taking, and a brilliant creative idea transformed the brand by celebrating the virtues of America's working class. "Miller Time," a simple, powerful creative image, transformed an inconsequential small business into a billion-a-year brand. Seventeen years later, when Miller abandoned the marketing idea, Budweiser took over the concept and executed it in a fresh way, and "This Bud's for You" produced many more billions of dollars.

And then there was Ray Kroc, a smart, genial man, who had the idea of creating a chain of clean, hospitable places where people could buy a burger and a drink—a place warmer and more charming than its main competitor, White Castle. But it wasn't until it encountered Keith Reinhard, a brilliant young writer at Needham, Harper & Steers in Chicago (the agency morphed into DDB Worldwide, and Keith became its legendary chairman) that McDonald's really took flight. Keith and his agency had an extraordinarily creative idea: to position McDonald's as an oasis for mothers and kids outside the home. They did this by "giving permission" for 1970s moms to take their kids out for lunch instead of cooking at home. The magical line "You Deserve a Break Today" helped put many billions of dollars of profit into the pockets of McDonald's shareholders.

With the same kind of simplicity and power, my friend Forest Long, a gifted writer and compassionate human being, came up with the unforgettable line "a mind is a terrible thing to waste" for the United Negro College Fund, helping put hundreds of millions of dollars behind the college educations for thousands of African American youths.

In all these instances, a creative idea fused—in the minds and hearts of customers—the identity of a brand with a way of life, an entire attitude toward one's own sense of worth. Creativity found a way for people to think in a new way about the importance of their own lives. Even in the humble context of selling hamburgers and beer, communication built around that purpose demonstrates creative insight's power to change the way people see their own lives. These advertising campaigns were early, rudimentary, and successful attempts to create an intimate relationship between a company and its customers, in ways that elevated the significance of a certain brand in that customer's life.

In today's world, we are witnessing many different and far more sophisticated forms of creativity at work in the field of marketing. I would characterize Dell as phenomenally successful at "applied creativity." It spends some $600 million a year to make highly technical improvements against highly segmented target groups: in other words it leverages innovations at Intel and others and finds creative ways to tailor that technology to the needs of specific groups of customers such as students. With individual customers, Dell puts creativity into their hands by allowing them to design their own computers online. At the end of the day, to its users, Dell is in perception and fact the best in the business, mostly because it has put creativity at the core of its relationship with its customers.

Creativity at Dell has evolved from something that works as the foundation of a marketing campaign into a spirit that lives in every interaction the company has with its customers.

The workhorse of the twenty-first century will be creativity, and management has to create an environment where people can be ready for—and working toward—the breakthrough idea. The question is how to foster the productive creativity needed to differentiate a brand in a surplus economy. America and the rest of the developed world must take note: creativity is the force without which our children won't enjoy a standard of living even remotely resembling ours. In the world of excess supply, natural resources, capital, and knowledge may let you make the cut into a global economic game—they won't enable you to win it. As I argued earlier, all these strengths will become commonplace, and where creativity doesn't drive a company's strategic vision, most often the lowest price will be the winning formula. Success, abundance, a rising standard of living—for individuals, companies, communities, nations—will depend on a capacity to create, invent, and innovate.

It comes down to an ability to differentiate your product or service in a relevant way. This leads inevitably to increased margins and profits. Without differentiation, we lapse back into a world of commodities. Outsourcing is a symptom of the new economic reality, a way of cutting costs in the face of brutal competition— inevitable if you are producing undifferentiated products and services and struggling against tighter margins. Your job, if it exists at all during the next decade, could be headed for India. Then it may move to Ghana. Start now. Differentiate yourself and your products. Get excited about what you're doing and add so much creativity and passion to what you do that nothing else compares with it. If you don't, nobody will care. Your job will evaporate.

I'm not talking about playtime. I'm talking about a work environment managed specifically to become a breeding ground for the prepared mind: a mind that seeks and finds creative solutions. Creativity doesn't mean entertainment, nor art. Unfettered creativity isn't the silver bullet. Applied, productive creativity with strategic value is the key—and that arises from immersion in the realities of challenges in the market. Before you can even think of doing something new, you need a comprehensive understanding of your businesses, products, and services as they exist today, a thorough understanding of how your organization is wired. Only with that as a foundation can a focused, productive creative energy lift an organization to the next level of practical, functional, and useful differentiation. You have not only to be good at the standard now, you have to understand the principles that have enabled you to succeed up to the present. Only then can you build on that foundation. Applied creativity needs to be fueled by knowledge of what is in order to get to what might be.

All this, again, only gets you onto the playing field. Once we qualify as competitors, we have to awaken and harness the creative power of everyone who contributes to an organized purpose. We need creativity aimed at a clearly defined target: the customer's heart. Learn creativity, teach it, and adapt it to every aspect of your waking life, because it isn't a "soft" subject anymore. It's the hardest core competency a business needs to develop.

The good news is, creativity is an inexhaustible, universal resource. It's as necessary as the air we breathe—and, luckily, it's almost as plentiful.

Creativity Is More Than a Gift

In business, creativity isn't a gift reserved for the guy in marketing communications with the earring, though he may have a head start on a certain kind of creativity. The sort I'm talking about here is a learned skill essential for everyone and every successful organization. I emphasize, it *can* be learned—even though creative insights aren't automatically predictable, repeatable, or rational. What's troubling, at first, is that these spontaneous insights are precisely what organizations need to survive now. You can learn to tap into your creativity again and again, but the creative act won't let itself be analyzed into submission. Rational thought, alone, will let you knock on the door of what's new, but it won't open that door.

Still, there's nothing occult or mystical about creativity. It's an innate human capacity, available to all healthy human beings. It is a neurological process, which, though it is yet to be fully understood or explained in scientific, technical terms, can be harnessed and nurtured. As elusive as it may seem, it's a skill available to all fully engaged, normal people.

Knocking on the Door

Before you even attempt to walk through the door into this new world of creativity, you have to find your way *to* it. This requires a few conditions:

- A rational, comprehensive understanding of the core business problem, need, or opportunity. This is crucial: it's where, having understood these elements of your situation, you can apply creativity to achieve productive *differentiation*.
- An intense, deep engagement with the task at hand. You have to immerse yourself in the issues before the spark of the new appears. You have to wallow in the facts, gain an understanding of conditions now. Understand *now* in order to see the *new*.
- Practice and refine the skill of finding patterns of unconnected events in the world of human experience. This can be learned.

Pattern recognition is one of the consistent elements of successfully creative business problem solvers. Insights can come from any direction if you hone this ability. Once, while reading an article in the *Washington Post* on the Aztec irrigation system that brought water to dry, barren fields in Mexico, I had a sudden recognition about how to help restructure my agency's direct marketing organization. Stories abound in business about how enormously successful products, from Post-it notes to Viagra, were discovered by seeing a popular application of something originally developed for a completely different purpose.

- Let creativity lead you in unexpected directions when it's strong. Discoveries in mathematics and in other fields offer many examples of the same kind of unexpected quality. If the discoverers hadn't been prepared to see the originality and use for the creative discovery, these products wouldn't exist— again, it depends on the ability to connect disparate patterns, see the application, and then *be willing to shift direction toward a new purpose and goal.*

- Learn to love the process of arriving at unusual, extraordinary solutions. Be willing to accept risk. A creative solution is almost always simple, but because it is different, it will always seem a bit risky to those around you. Learn to live with that.

It has become a truism that creative insight originates most often in the right hemisphere of the brain, while the left hemisphere governs rational thought. Both are essential in solving dramatically different kinds of problems. Researchers Michael Ray and Rochelle Myers, authors of *Creativity in Business*, who offer a course of the same name at Stanford School of Business, claim the *entire* brain comes into play during moments of intense creativity— including the limbic brain and brain stem, structures that reach back through eons of evolution. These findings show that creativity is an innate, biologically governed human activity. The question is how to encourage and integrate this individual biological process into larger organizational patterns.

It's a tough but critical question. Few of us have been educated to be creative. Sadly, in America and other developed countries today, across most of our educational curriculum, the emphasis is almost exclusively on the logical and rational—skills as consistently repeatable as the sum of two plus two, necessary but hardly sufficient. What we teach our children, what we learn ourselves, is rarely anchored in an understanding of art, music, higher mathematics, or any of the other intuitive, nonlinear, and creative human achievements. This has to change. We must consciously decide to develop the brain's whole capability and allow it to come into play. Secondary school leadership and higher education must help our next generations be better prepared to use their whole brains, not only for artistic development but also for everyday business. It is tragic to see in our times the first thing to be cut from public schools across the country is almost any form of art, music, and the other studies that nurture the creative process.

Up against the sort of thinking our schools turn out year after year, it's no wonder business rarely operates to cultivate creativity, but instead reproduces environments inadvertently designed to stifle it. Once you understand how the brain becomes creative and what surroundings nourish that skill, you'll begin to see why organizations need to operate in new and different ways.

The Creative Cauldron

But before getting to that, it may help to show what science has established about the origins of creativity. Creative acts happen in a particular, well-defined state of mind. This has been simply demonstrated by hooking the brain to an electroencephalograph and monitoring electrical impulses during a subject's creative activity. As it turns out, the human brain's electromagnetic frequency can be broken into four kinds of wave patterns: beta, alpha, theta, and delta. The beta state, the brain's highest brain frequency, is where we spend the vast majority of our conscious time: the average waking state. It involves the cacophony of multiple stimuli and is least conducive to creativity. Alpha, by contrast, is the twilight between full consciousness and sleep, the golden hour, the most fertile state for the brain. Interestingly, it is the state of mind where children exist up to the ages of seven or eight. This, in part, explains why children are so prone to fantasy and play, free-association and intuition. Theta and delta are the lowest frequency levels, where some extraordinarily creative people and some religious luminaries, including the Dalai Lama, have been found to exist in a conscious level. Theta and delta for most people are the brain frequencies emitted during the most healthful sleep time of their lives—and aren't of interest to us here. It's the alpha state an organization wants to cultivate if it hopes to encourage widespread creativity.

People whose consciousness is in an alpha state are, almost inevitably, more creative, more imaginative. It isn't something reserved for the lucky few. A vast amount of literature describes how people find their own instinctive ways to get into an alpha state other than sleep. It takes practice. The most common and healthful way to achieve an alpha state is some form of meditation—focused, purposeful relaxation. There are many forms—yoga, Zen, simple breathing exercises—meditation is no more exotic than creativity itself. It's a natural, simple way to achieve an alpha state while conscious, on an individual level.

Having worked with thousands of creative people, I've seen some unusual, idiosyncratic ways of getting into this state of mental flow. One fellow I worked with would drink a glass of warm water: that's all it took to ignite his creative firepower, as he put it. Another visualized lowering himself into a well where, deep down, toward the bottom of the well, he found the source of his inspiration. There were other practical solutions: rocking in an easy chair, a rhythmic motion that stimulated new ideas, and obviously brought back memories of that continuous alpha state of childhood. Still others looked deep into space with their eyes aimed upward at a 45-degree angle.

These are all individual efforts. I have experienced such moments myself and have observed them many times in business. Organizations magnify individual creativity through collaboration, partnerships, brainstorming sessions, late-night teamwork, all of which produce an exponential enhancement of each individual's productivity. As an example, in the advertising industry, "creative teams"—those people who produce the actual commercials—are always paired up, a writer working with an art director. Early in my career, I considered this unproductive. It seemed, well, *expensive*. My thinking was simple. Most writers I knew could draw and art directors could write—and this, it seemed, offered room to cut costs and improve productivity. What I came to realize was that something else was at work here, the interaction between two creative minds, which seemed to work in practical reality better than a single mind. Literature about fifth-generation computers, yet to arrive, describes a parallel processing model that adds exponentially to what a single processor can do, regardless of its size. There may well be a useful analogy here: the outcome of collaborative efforts is far greater than the sum of the individual minds involved. The writer–art director pairing was in fact an investment in a greater, more rewarding creative output. Every business should seek and find opportunities to create collaborative environments that produce more creative results. The effort and investment is likely to be rewarded exponentially.

Creative Collaboration

If you are running an organization or a department or a small office, you can't simply tell your people to relax in their own way, cross their eyes, drink some warm water, slip into an alpha state, and come up with the Next Big Thing in time for lunch. In business, the energy of all those individual brains is a fragile organizational resource. It needs to be supported, nurtured, and husbanded—and that is precisely where the demand for creativity requires a completely new approach to running organizations. You can't force it to appear. You can't intimidate insights out of people. As noted, children are naturally in an alpha state up until the age of about seven or eight. Why does it begin to erode? There may be biological reasons, but it's probably no coincidence that around that age children have been going to school long enough to feel the pull of a much colder, much riskier world outside their home. The nurturing, loving environment of home has a much smaller reach than it used to, for them. Anxiety begins to replace trust and affection. Work begins to supplant play as a primary activity.

The question is how to get the spirit of play, the relaxed and confident delight in new ideas, back into the act of working—especially when, all along, an organization faces gathering pressure from growing competition and all the forces of market erosion in the excess supply world. The key is for leadership to keep in mind that there's a direct link between creative confidence and market differentiation. Leadership in a successful business now requires a skill set grounded in a respectful understanding of the creative process and willing to provide the environment needed to sustain creativity. (Chapter Three deals with this in even more detail.)

The simple fact remains that an alpha-like state of mind is essential for the creative process to happen—and that nothing disrupts it like the classic management techniques that have worked for so many centuries: bullying command-and-control, motivation through fear. You'll get obedience. You'll get uniform productivity in familiar ways. But you won't get the kind of daily, hourly inventiveness so vital to success now. That requires a congenial, supporting environment.

On the other hand, creativity shouldn't be babied. As fragile as it is, creativity is inexhaustible. The more you use it, the stronger and more plentiful it gets. Of all the resources available in excess now, creativity is the most abundant. And it emerges only through hard work. It requires the confidence to reach deep within, assured that going through the creative process is the only path to a distinctive, unique, and differentiating solution. If you've defined the problem and done all the work toward understanding the needs, with collaborative creativity the moment will arrive when the solution will occur. It can't be forced. But it does show up, very often to the prepared mind, the one who has gone through the discipline of preparing for it.

One can and must set high aspirations for output—and hold it to firm measures of its effectiveness. Focus creativity to solve highly specific problems. Managers who understand and respect creative power—how to manage it, how to harness it to produce results—will become leaders, and their organizations winning enterprises by standing out against a competitive environment that commoditizes everything but the most differentiated products and services.

Because organizational creativity requires collaboration and the ability to function in creative mind states, which involves the need to take risks and accept rejection, the creative environment becomes critical in optimizing productive creative output. That environment must have all these features:

- A clear set of goals and aspirations that are measurable.
- A supportive culture that provides clear and complete information to the creative person and team.
- An encouraging environment that allows for risk taking, along with some inevitable failure and rejection.
- A reward system both financial and emotional that is tied to measurable results.

For many years, creativity and nurturing work environments were considered "soft" topics. The let's-get-busy-we've-got-work-to-do taskmasters had little time for the notion of zany dreamers the word *creative* often evoked. But no more. Playful, surprising, unpredictable—these adjectives were all anathema to the traditional business environment—and still are, in many cases. They were all characteristics of human behavior that would have led to failure in a rigorous industrial assembly-line culture. But not now. It's a new world. In the world of excess supply, where everything ripens into a commodity given enough time, creativity is tomorrow's factory for sustainable success.

Now we have entire industries totally dependent on continuous innovation: blue chips like Intel, Microsoft, Xerox, IBM, and the pharmaceutical companies, which spend individually in the billions on research and development. In academic medical centers, clinical innovation is de rigueur. More than that, all companies in tomorrow's world will have to think of innovation and differentiation as the staple of their business or else their jobs will go to India, China, and then Ghana or Zaire. Anywhere but here. Creativity must be embraced by all schools, from primary to graduate, all businesses, and even government. Creativity is serious business.

It has always been serious business for me. In advertising, creativity is most indispensable when you are trying to win new business. Clients in need of urgent solutions to serious problems go looking for a new creative spark, and that's when you have to shine—when you are proving yourself to someone who doesn't know you. It's obvious how this has become crucial for all organizations, since the act of proving oneself to a customer has become a daily necessity—you have to approach existing customers, now, as if you're winning new business. Winning new loyal customers is when you must lean more heavily on differentiation: if you don't stand out in a clear, relevant way, you won't even get noticed.

Creativity Grows from the Mission

Apple Computer ranks as one of the most creative organizations to spring up in the past fifty years, even though it isn't a classic case history in how to succeed. It has hobbled itself with bad strategic marketing decisions as it has grown, yet it continues to innovate in a way that inspires its tiny segment of devoted customers—who aren't just satisfied with the product. They are virtually members of a cult. Steven Wozniak joined Steve Jobs, in Jobs's garage, to assemble their Apple I, designing it in six months and building it in forty hours, introducing it in the mid-1970s, and then coming out a year later with the Apple II, fixing nearly everything that hadn't worked in the first model. After two years, the company employed 250 people, on a path of astonishing growth. Apple's story underscores two vital points. The importance of constant creative effort and innovation and the critical role of a new kind of leadership that enables creativity to become a core competence. The leadership topic is explored in more detail in Chapter Three.

Like Xerox, from which Apple learned, some would say heavily borrowed, all the basics of the graphical user interface with which Apple revolutionized personal computing—windows, mouse, pulldown menus, and icons—it was unable to see that to achieve its goal of making computers a household appliance, its own product would have to become a commodity. Bill Gates, at Microsoft, took the same innovations, opened up the secrets of his operating system and licensed them out to any other company that wanted to build its own hardware or software around it, and quickly came to dominate the computer market.

The leaders at Apple understood clearly that to stay in business, the company had to do more than sell a fine commodity computer at ever decreasing margins. Apple would thrive only by creating new benefits, through new improvements, with regularity.

The spirit of creativity is as strong as ever at Apple—and there is a charm, a friendliness, and beauty to everything Apple does that is light-years beyond the omnipresent PC world. To a great degree, that charm, the aura of something absolutely special and rare—the antithesis of the excess supply realities—can be traced to the culture created by Steve Jobs. When he returned to Apple, the company launched the iPod, which has become the new standard for portable music players—with an almost magical design that inspires the same kind of religious fervor among its users. This is creativity as its best: innovation that connects with individual customers and ignites fierce loyalty to the brand, using the most subtle design inflections to build its fortress in the hearts of its users. The stories of Apple's internal culture are plentiful, and even the language used to describe the company's operations ring with a sense of mission: it employs evangelists, not sales reps. When Jobs hired John Sculley away from Pepsi, he won Sculley over by asking, "Do you want to sell sugar water to kids for the rest of your life or do you want to change the world?"

Many tales, good and bad, of how Apple's sense of mission generated amazing creative advances—which weren't always backed up by the best business plan or marketing strategy—can be found at the Web log for Apple history at the Computer History Museum Web site. One story from the site tells of how the company's research operation in Cambridge, Massachusetts, which had developed a new product called Dylan, was disbanded. It gave the staff *six months' notice* to find jobs. The good will and compassion of this gesture wasn't lost on the workers. Everyone printed T-shirts with the names of everyone being laid off, and on the day of the layoffs they decorated the office with Halloween fare, including an animatronic raven and apple turnovers for refreshments. As the final meeting was convened, and the human resource people called them all up for a folder of layoff paperwork, the whole group applauded each worker as he or she walked up to receive the proverbial pink slip.

That kind of spirit is the whole point: it's the sort of culture that nurtures creativity at every level and in every worker. The key is to cultivate a spirit, a sense that every gesture, every word, contributes to a company's unique mission—across an organization by maintaining a culture where people feel eager and proud to come into work every day, where people believe they are doing something in a way that no other company can quite match, even if the market share doesn't measure up to the dream. It's an organization where people are constantly thinking of brighter ways to do what seems ordinary in other companies—including a celebration of their own job loss.

The Softer Side of Sears

In the early 1990s, Sears needed a makeover. The brand was stale. To most people, the name meant metal and wood and copper wire—hammers and pliers, car batteries, refrigerators, and barbecue grills. It was an accurate perception, up to a point. Appliances dominated the Sears product line, and this was both a strength and a weakness. Profit margins were razor-thin, because price comparisons were so easy to make and because the so-called category-killer retailers (Home Depot, The Wiz, Circuit City, and so on) had made steeply discounted prices on such items into an everyday way of life. Sears was blending into the market, becoming nearly invisible to customers who had more and more choices for the same kind of retail convenience.

When Arthur Martinez became CEO of Sears in 1995, he saw all this and—with the full backing of his board of directors—acted on it immediately. In his book, *The Hard Road to the Softer Side*, he recounts how he transformed and revived the company by remaking his brand. Young & Rubicam, along with a variety of other agencies, entered a grueling five-month competition for the Sears account. We invested close to $2 million in the process. What enabled us to enter into this competition with confidence was the way we'd organized ourselves, according to the principles of this book, so that we all worked in an environment where people knew how to lay the creative groundwork for a breakthrough idea to emerge. In retrospect, this effort was a test case in whether or not an organization can turn itself into an incubator of strategically creative insight while following what have become the principles of this book.

Over the preceding three years, every business magazine had published a cover story predicting the death of Sears. Martinez considered the reports a bit premature. With a little help from Y&R, he proved them all wrong, taking Sears into one of the most famous corporate turnarounds ever. He invited all the leading ad agencies in America to propose their visions of how to bring more customers to the Sears apparel business. The agency with the most powerful solution would win the account—worth many millions of dollars a year.

We were thrilled to be invited into the competition. We sensed it could become the culmination of our long-standing ambition to do business with Sears, historically one of the ten biggest advertisers in the world. Hardware was the company's cash cow. We imagined a parade of men passing blindly through the lingerie department on their way to buy a garbage disposal. The trick was to do just the opposite: bring their wives through the appliance department on their way to buy shoes. We needed those women to know it was just as fine a place to buy skirts and sweaters. Stephie Kugelman, one of the key members of the Y&R team, was the one who squeezed the challenge into a nutshell. She said: "It felt like trying to convince someone to buy a party dress at a hardware store."

We assembled a team of high-powered talent: Stephie, and Frank Anfield, then head of our New York office, and New York creative director Helene Spivak, and several others, including Jim Hood, head of new business at that time, and two creative directors, Deborah Stern and Tom Shortledge. Each was and is not only a gifted professional but a unique and valuable personality.

We embarked on a long process: months of inventing, testing, massaging, and trashing one idea after another. Our team spent early mornings, most nights, and most weekends working on the project. We started with an enormous data dump. We'd brought home from Chicago reams of numbers and facts about Sears, its customers, its competitors, and trends in apparel. We synthesized and studied all of it, trying to sharpen our understanding of the target market and what it would take to reach it. For the duration of the contest, one conference room at Y&R became the Sears Room, and the team was quarantined there, late at night, on weekends, around the clock, struggling to get a handle on the challenge—and we all had "day jobs," a full workload of our regular account business, to do at the same time.

A new supply of pizza and cola arrived every couple of hours. We lived for days at a time on carbs and caffeine. As we studied and restudied the research, debated conclusions, and argued ideas, we laughed constantly. It was a riot, most of the time—pure fun. Inside those doors, no idea was too ridiculous or stupid to voice. No one was allowed to pull rank. Unless everyone felt appreciated and supported—free to be creative without risk—we never would have discovered a way to turn Sears around.

Stephie, an elegant, soft-spoken woman with an unparalleled knowledge of the American consumer, who later became CEO of Y&R's New York office, suggested conducting an in-depth study of our target customers—middle-American working women. They weren't a monolithic group. Some were single, some married; some were mothers, some not. Some but not all were "career women." Stephanie sensed that the key to creating effective advertising for this group lay in fully understanding these women and their lives, dreams, problems, and motivations. Once we could do that, we could pull them through the doors in great numbers.

We jumped on Stephie's idea and assembled a cadre of trained psychologists, researchers, and cameramen. It was costly, but we knew it was also an essential financial risk: we had to invest money in this research effort to come up with an idea that was rooted in reality. We sent them out to homes across the country to literally spend a week living with real-life Sears customers. Like anthropologists studying some remote Pacific tribe, they filled notebooks with observations, conducted long (and often surprisingly revealing) interviews, and produced hundreds of hours of videotape. The results were eye-opening and remarkable. We listened closely to the presentations of the researchers, trying to find the knowledge we needed to chart a new path for Sears.

We read their reports and watched excerpts from their films, and a powerful portrait of the Sears customers emerged. We discovered that these women were both very ordinary and very special. They loved their families passionately and wanted more than anything to provide their kids and their spouses with rich, rewarding lives and all the benefits the modern world has to offer, from ballet and piano lessons for the kids to nice homes with comfortable, inviting furnishings to a fun, relaxing family vacation once or twice a year. These are simple aspirations, but they cost money and require lots of hard work. And these women did work hard—day and night, weekdays and weekends, on the job and at home. They were master jugglers, brilliantly balancing family obligations, civic responsibilities, work demands, and time for themselves, somehow managing to keep it all under control (most of the time).

The more we learned about these women, the more we liked and admired them—and the more we respected them. They did everything their male counterparts did and a lot more. Perhaps most remarkable of all was their humility. As the interviews made clear, these working women took their lives in stride and seemed to be enjoying themselves. In the end, all of this research was distilled into a forty-minute film that was amazing and inspirational to watch. It helped us understand what Sears—and our agency—had to live up to.

But what crystallized and electrified the team—what completely changed our understanding of the challenge ahead of us—was a single number, buried deep in the research. One day, one of the team members held up a sheet of paper: "Look at this. This'll blow you away." We passed around the passage he'd highlighted. It was quite simple. It said, "Eighty-four percent of all purchases at Sears, of all goods, are made by women."

None of us ever would have guessed anything close to that number. We had pounds and pounds of data on paper, but this little number lurked in only one place in all those stacks of print-outs, and somehow we'd been lucky enough to spot it. All this information—women liked this, women liked that, but none of it was as forceful as this figure. We didn't have to draw women through the doors. They were flooding through the doors already. Women *controlled* Sears. Women were the power. We'd imagined a parade of men going in and out of the store carrying Craftsman power drills, lawn mowers, and faucets. But no. It had been women, even for most of the hardware purchases. This astounded us. Our target audience was already *there,* inside the building. They just weren't buying apparel. Any campaign for Sears, for *any* product— from car batteries to sandals—had to use this knowledge to direct its approach to these women. It changed our entire mind-set and gave us the incentive and focus we needed. Women were already in the building: they simply needed to understand what Sears could offer them while they were there.

If we'd ever been tempted to condescend to the Sears customer, the research blew away any such thinking. These women were smart and sophisticated—true CEOs of their households—able, hard-working women with tastes and desires for things considered strictly feminine. And that, precisely, was what Sears needed to tap—their feminine side—without ignoring all the rest that we'd learned about them. Based on these findings, we created a one-page strategy document with which we briefed a collection of ten teams, each including a writer and an art director, whose job was to take our insights to the next level.

For several weeks, Helene Spivak—funny and slightly sarcastic, a short, prickly achiever, a New Yorker to the core—worked closely with a multitude of teams. Periodically, Helene, Stephie, Frank, Jim, and I would gather to listen to the various teams put forth their ideas. We asked the teams to come back with a summary line—a slogan summarizing the positioning of Sears. We were inundated with hundreds of lines, all intelligently crafted but most just slightly off-target, usually in very subtle ways. One whole series of ideas started with the established Sears image—hardware and the like— and then went on to say: *There's more to Sears than this*. The trick was to come up with a line that said this with more emotional impact and without sounding negative.

So we heard lines like, "Sears is more than hardware," and "Sears for your hammer, your refrigerator, and so much more." There was nothing really bad about these approaches, but they had no soul. And we were worried about denigrating the traditional Sears store or making it seem secondary—as if there were something wrong with being "just hardware." The same was true of the lives of the women who shopped there—we didn't want to dismiss their own hard-nosed character, the way they worked for living successfully in what had previously been a man's world, and the way they came to Sears for appliances and hardware. Instead, we wanted to acknowledge the familiar (and respected) aspects of Sears while introducing and celebrating a whole new element. For the same reason, lines like: "Now Sears is a fashion store" struck the wrong balance. We didn't want to imply Sears had changed. After all, Sears had been selling clothing forever.

There was a third direction that felt almost right—but not quite. Some suggested we emphasize the "middle-American" part of the customer equation. Why not play off this just-plain-folks image by using a line like "Sears is the store for you," or "Sears, the fabric of America." With her deep insight into customers—and enlightened by our research studies into the Sears woman—Stephie was able to steer us firmly away from the dangers of this approach. "Remember," she warned us, "the Sears woman isn't living under a mushroom somewhere. Sure, she's hard-working, without pretense, and so on. But she has a sense of style. She wants to look good for her husband or for her friends. She may not get her tastes from runway models but she wants to buy clothes that will help her look and feel pretty and feminine."

"Somehow," Stephanie concluded, "we have to show her that Sears is offering real style—but without overdoing it, so that customers don't get the idea that the Sears they love is being transformed into some kind of high-priced, high-fashion store. She likes Sears. She just doesn't realize that it has a feminine side."

We kept getting closer to the answer. One suggestion was so good, we were dying to use it—*Sears, we're changing our gear*—but it wasn't quite right. Finally, Sue Reed, a brilliant writer, came up with the ultimate solution, the Grail of our quest. She knew we needed to celebrate the feminine side of Sears while playfully winking at the familiar, masculine side and denigrating neither.

"I have a very simple way to celebrate this woman, this feminine, harassed, busy woman, the CEO of the household," she said. "I have the way to get this target customer's trust."

"Okay. Shoot."

She held up a card. On it were only five words: *The Softer Side of Sears*.

Stephie, Frank, Helene and I jumped up at once. Stephie and Frank literally ran around the table to give Sue a hug.

Our search was over. This was the Eureka moment. Months of working into the night and on weekends, millions of dollars of investment in research, all that effort had come down to those five magic words. It's frightening, in retrospect, to realize how uncertain, how risky, all that preparation and investment had been. It's the terrible truth of all creativity: you can work days, months, years, and yet, no matter how hard you work, nothing will guarantee those five words, or their equivalent, at the end of your journey. Either you dis-cover the magic or you don't. There is no repeatable way to do it. You can create a garden where things like this will be more likely to bloom, but genuine creativity is the most uncertain, unpredictable, unrepeatable phenomenon in all of business—in all of human experience—even though it has become the root of all success.

Debra Stern and Tom Shortledge took the line and worked on how to craft it in advertising, executions as innovative as the line itself: surprising, dramatic, new ways to look at the promise, the benefit. Trying to identify and evoke in an emotional, memo-rable way what the apparel section represented within the Sears store, they suggested pairing traditional Sears hard goods with a soft goods side. Thus, a garden hose and a water pump would morph into an attractive model in stylish stockings ("hose") and sling-back high heels ("pumps"). This was great, original thinking, classic advertising. We were running on all eight cylinders now.

So when the time came to bring our ideas to Sears, we decided to stake everything on the Softer Side. It isn't unusual for an agency to offer several alternative campaigns, but we decided to present nothing but this core idea. In Chicago, we assembled all our final materials—slides, handouts, animatics (animated story boards with sound tracks for showing on a TV monitor)—and checked them, double-checked them, and rehearsed. Finally, at the appointed hour, we presented our idea to the Sears team—sixteen executives, led, of course, by Arthur Martinez himself, along with two members of the consulting team. We showed a long excerpt from our film of the heroic Sears customer and then explained our thinking about Sears and the Sears apparel marketing challenge in detail, culmi-nating with the Softer Side line and the sample executions.

It's rare that you can tell right away how fully you've connected with your audience at a session like this one. In this case, we felt we got a good reaction, but we left the room uncertain as to whether we'd hit a home run or not. We were soon to learn Sears chose Y&R, and the customers loved the Softer Side campaign. Sales at Sears improved dramatically from the first week the commercials aired. "The campaign hit faster than anything anyone had ever seen," Martinez recalls in *The Hard Road to the Softer Side*. "It was the right message at the right time."

The Softer Side campaign energized Sears associates as well as consumers and moved the business forward for several years. If we, or our competitive agencies, hadn't come up with the relevant and differentiating campaign, one of the world's great retailers might have closed its doors. Instead, we found just the right combination of words, images, music, and ideas to give Sears a fresh new look and offer customers new motivation to come through the doors and spend money. It took millions of dollars, thousands of hours, and the passion of an entire organization working as a team, and what won the day was a completely original, creative idea—a mere five words—that helped generate millions in profits.

The hero of the Sears story was creativity itself, driven by the rigorous, disciplined passion to serve a client. That inventiveness never would have emerged without the leadership of Arthur Martinez: a shining example of a man who ran his company by strong, fundamental values. Of course, advertising was only a part of the Sears turnaround. New, more fashionable merchandising, a better trained group of associates, better displays, eventually better-lit, improved stores were part of that effort. But without those five words, no one would have noticed the changes or cared much about the new fixtures.

The Softer Side campaign generated remarkable results. The marketing research showed that women—once the Softer Side brought them into the store—would want to shop and buy products from tables, so the corporation invested $4.5 million in tables for the selling floor. As Martinez wrote in his book: "We sold hundreds of millions worth of items from that $4.5 million table investment in just *the first two months*." Ultimately, the campaign generated billions in market capitalization for the company. The stock price almost doubled. Also as a part of the new campaign, Sears developed its own line of clothing brands, to appeal to the new shoppers coming into the store. "That business amounted to $300 million in the first year, then jumped to $900 million and is now at the $2 billion level." In other words, the results of Martinez's leadership during that crucial period—founded on a creative approach to the customer that differentiated the brand in a relevant way—were staggering. The power of the creative idea, embodied in nothing more than five words, transformed and revitalized an entire corporation.

3

ENLIGHTENED LEADERSHIP

No More Mr. Tough Guy

I'd just gotten a big promotion, maybe a stepping stone to even greater future responsibilities. I was a smart advertising executive, though I was far from the smartest at Y&R. My success had come from helping and encouraging others more talented than I was—writers, artists, marketing strategists—in creating brand-building ideas for our clients. I knew that much of my success would depend on one of my direct reports, a fellow I'll call Mike.

Both Mike and I were Y&R lifers. We got along well. He was big, jovial, funny, and emotional in a good way—full of charm. He came from Connecticut, very Catholic, always an account guy. He started in New York in research, as I did, but he was on a faster growth curve and he moved around to different offices without hesitation. He'd joined Young & Rubicam some years before me.

I thought I'd always be lower than he was on the organization chart. Yet eventually, as I began to move up at Y&R, I leapfrogged Mike. I went from being one of his team to being his boss. Even though his seniority meant that Mike made more money than I did even when he was working *for* me, the way I passed him in my career dealt a hard blow to his ego.

In the past, Mike and I had always worked well together. We'd been congenial and mutually supportive. I assumed Mike would give me the same kind of loyalty now that our roles were reversed. But it wasn't so. Soon after I was promoted over him, people said Mike was trying to undermine me. Mike denied it.

"Peter," he assured me, "you and I go back too far together for you to believe such silliness. There must be some misunderstanding. Believe me, I'll clear it up right away."

But in the weeks that followed, the undercurrent of tension throughout the business deepened and spread. People began to accuse me of being shallow, a technocrat, and (worst of all), "anti-creative." That stung in a business like advertising, where the only real product is creativity. It was true that I didn't want award-winning work at any cost to the client: I wanted award-winning creativity that had strategic power.

"I'll commit any atrocity," Mike once declared, "in the service of great creative work."

This kind of grandstanding worked. It rallied a large portion of the creative staff against me. The writers and artists cheered him on. It threw me into a state of intense, chronic questioning and self-doubt. He was lying to me and lying about me to others, yet, face to face, he acted as if we were the same old pals. The only way he could behave this way, do what he felt he had to do to survive, psychologically—to fight the feeling of being a failure, by comparison with me—was to attack me and yet deny he was doing it, even to himself.

Eventually, I had to quit making excuses for him. One option, of course, was simply to fire Mike. But I couldn't bring myself to do it. Mike wasn't himself anymore. I wanted to protect him from *himself* in the process of saving my career. Mike was an asset. We needed him. I struggled for months, virtually on my own. Although I was supposed to be Mike's manager, in fact Mike was managing *me*.

The quality of our creative work began to slip. I felt a deepening sense of pain, humiliation, and frustration. I felt everything I'd achieved in my life beginning to slip away. My wife, Barbara, was worried about me. And through it all, a deep-seated feeling of resentment, even rage, was slowly building inside me.

All through the experience I kept holding out hope that Mike could *evolve*. I hoped he could wake up to the reality of his actions and change as a person. But finally, after an entire year of watching this contest degenerate and eat away at both morale and the quality of our work, I couldn't stand it. The company had recruited me, trained me, supported me, and helped me develop into a mature professional and now it was letting me down. I was ready to quit.

Instead, I talked to my boss, laid out the problem, and got his total support. I called Mike in. I told him, in detail, what he'd been doing and why it could no longer be tolerated. I went through it with the sort of precision he couldn't simply shrug off. I didn't yell. My only focus was to get to the truth, and then go from there. It changed everything. Mike astonished me with his honesty and courage.

"You're right," he said. "That's exactly what I've been doing. You have every right to fire me. I deserve that. But before you do, let me ask you to consider something. I've spent so many good years in this company. For most of that time, I've given Y&R my best. I cared for our clients. I got results for them. So here's what I can offer. You guys give me the ugliest problem in the company, anywhere in the world, and I'll fix your problem—and then I can leave this place with my head high. Last, let me tell you this, Peter. You'll never have to watch your back. Never. Not only that, I'll be your most loyal and trusted advocate and supporter."

I looked Mike in the eye, I told him, "If you really mean it, you've got a deal." We shook hands, and we hugged.

"It's your call," he said. "I'll go along with whatever you decide."

In the end, we gave Mike a job worthy of his talents and ability. A tough and demanding job. A challenge critical to the company's success. Mike took to the assignment with enthusiasm and relish. He did a great job. He got results. He, indeed, became my most loyal and ardent supporter, until he chose to retire.

Unlikely as it may seem, Mike became one of the colleagues I admired most. He changed. He demonstrated he could be trusted. I was wise not to move too quickly and fire Mike in the early days of his misbehavior. I was wrong in waiting so long for a serious confrontation with him. But the biggest insight I've drawn from the episode is that grown adults can change—if they are smart enough, wise enough, courageous enough. It turned out Mike was a big man, the good man he'd always been. He became one my heroes. He achieved a new kind of humility and evolved beyond his own most destructive instincts. He proved what I'd believed all along. It's possible for a human being to evolve. Mike did, and maybe I did too, in the ordeal of that trial.

In this new century, a new kind of enlightened leadership will transform the way we all do business. Only enlightened leadership can cultivate and nurture the sort of work environment where prepared minds are working toward the creative breakthroughs needed to rise above the surplus economy. It will replace the familiar sort of tough-guy commander with a more intelligent, supple, and responsive kind of leader. Down through history, the mean-spirited tough guy has generally been either a clever thief or a bully. Both of these types have been admired, envied, feared, and obeyed—and with good reason. They've gotten results. Now, both forms of tough-guy leadership have become timeworn and, ultimately, destructive.

The thief has become all too familiar of late and has been thoroughly discredited. No one tolerates dishonesty in business with a wink and a nudge anymore. We've seen enough CEOs doing the perp walk in cuffs, appearing for arraignment and trial, for the lesson to stick—they've been branded as villains instead of secretly admired for their ability to play the system. Yet laws alone won't prevent this kind of bad faith: the government can't police every boardroom and annual report. Only a voluntary adherence to honest principles will build integrity and trust. With the collapse of trust, the system of free enterprise crashes. If the numbers don't mean anything, then all confidence is lost.

There's some seriously good news hidden away behind the headlines, though. In my forty years in business, I have worked with thousands of leaders and hundreds of companies and all the major accounting firms, and I have found extraordinarily honest people who care deeply and passionately about doing things with integrity and honesty. It is a relatively small but high-profile group of thieves who have been rooted out over the past few years and must continue to be identified and branded—the exceptions to the rule have given the world of business a bad name. The system wouldn't have worked at all until now if this weren't true.

The bully is still tolerated, to a degree. There remains, in some quarters, an enduring admiration for Machiavellian realpolitik in the practice of making money: it's a tough, brutal world and, until recently, the toughest, most cunning leaders were often the winners. When things started to get tougher—during the last decade, and especially over the past few years—the impulse was to do what always worked before: be ruthless, cut jobs, and instill fear as a motivator. Toughness has always been a badge of superiority in business—and tough decision making is essential to success. But it shouldn't be mistaken for the cruel, mean-spirited ignorance of those who abuse people to extort obedience. Toughness, in practice, can take on a darker meaning: a poisonous worship of winning at any cost, with a corresponding debasement of values. This misdirected toughness, over the last decade, in too many cases degenerated into cynical self-interest and a kind of survivalist greed. It meant lining your own pockets and getting out—often in perfectly legal ways—and leaving the riddles of a new century's economy for someone else to figure out.

The Clever Thieves

In the old economic world of scarcity, the clever thieves—the robber barons, the brutal and oppressive builders of the free world's industrial might—found they could get results with deceit, manipulation, and an iron fist. Now the thieves grab headlines with their crimes rather than their accomplishments. The stories of thousands of people at Enron and Anderson who worked their whole lives in good faith, only to find their dreams shattered by their leaders' greed—these tales are enough to make many people view everyone in business as a potential criminal.

When top executives at companies—such as Adelphia, the nation's sixth-largest cable operator, WorldCom, the global communications giant, and Conseco, a financial corporation with $94 billion in managed assets—arranged for massive personal loans backed by their companies, it should have meant only one thing to anyone who saw it happening: these leaders saw the end coming and were cashing in on the way out. Dennis Kozlowski, former chairman and chief executive of Tyco International—and one of the highest-paid executives in the country—was indicted in Manhattan on charges of evading more than $1 million of sales taxes on six paintings that he bought for $13.1 million for his thirteen-room apartment on Fifth Avenue. Others, such as Gary Winnick of Global Crossing, Joe Nacchio of Qwest, and Ken Lay of Enron, extracted hundreds of millions of dollars from their corporations by selling shares before their stock crashed, leaving millions of investors holding the bag.

For CEOs to claim ignorance of what was happening in their own organizations—as many have done—is outrageous, and a mark of how brazen dishonesty at the top can become. It has extended itself well beyond those who, in apprehension, see the end of a good thing and want to gain as much as possible, by whatever means, before things fall apart. At Enron, some of what top executives did was apparently legal, but it wasn't right. The stock rose in price because of a vast web of collaboration and deception, a willing suspension of disbelief, if you will, among a large array of people, all of whom had a stake in propping up the price of Enron stock. John

Ellis took an extreme position when he pointed out (in the May 2002 issue of *Fast Company* magazine) that the real culprit in the Enron scandal was Wall Street. He spoke for a growing number of people who view business with cynicism:

"The larger, more important story is the whole culture of dishonesty on what we call Wall Street. It starts with a lie. Earnings don't mean anything; they can be engineered. It is seconded by another lie: Those financially engineered numbers are right. It is complicated by yet more lies: Sales revenue and cash flow can be manipulated as well. And then it is all locked down in a code of omerta: *Enron is a strong buy.*"

This sort of willingness to go to any length to be a winner isn't restricted to business, obviously. Every two years, whether it's the summer or winter Olympics, we see the same phenomenon, the desperate sickness to win at any cost, where educated athletes (like their counterparts in business) attempt to take away the gold by any means, including the risk of destroying their reputations, careers, and long-term health by abusing illegal drugs. The baseball steroid saga is yet another sad tale. It's a part of human nature: the craving to survive translated into the terms of a game.

Because human nature has a bias toward these instincts, organizations need to create a culture that doesn't reward but shuns and weeds out behavior governed by them. The Sarbanes-Oxley Act of 2002 went a long way toward bringing confidence and trust back into the system. Now, the CEO and CFO have to sign off on financial statements. Boards of directors must take responsibility for overseeing the culture of the company and making sure it represents good values to the best of its ability. In company after company, now, second-tier managers talk openly about these kinds of issues with a renewed sense of commitment. But, ultimately, enlightened leadership is the answer: the ability of those in charge to resist the urge to win at any cost.

Meet the Classic Bully

The second type, the bullies, are subversive. Even though their ability to do harm is great, this type is still widely, and mistakenly, admired. Their style has lost both its cruel charm and its effectiveness.

Al Dunlap was a good example. He straddled both roles. He made millions using slash-and-burn tactics to "save" troubled companies—coming in, getting tough, doing the dirty work, and everyone would applaud. *Somebody had to do it.* But then the truth came out, and his shady accounting tricks finally brought him down. Even at lower levels of an organization, managers who operate by the sort of primitive instincts that used to be the hallmark of the captain of industry can cause serious damage, measured in careers spoiled, reputations shattered, and relationships broken.

The Bully isn't, by definition, dishonest—*outdated* is a better designation. Carly Fiorina, the dismissed CEO of Hewlett-Packard, is a good example. The moment she entered the corporation, lambasting and firing division heads for doing badly, the handwriting was on the wall. She joined HP after leaving Lucent, a spin-off of AT&T, where she'd had a long career. Within the first six months of her arrival at her new West Coast job, she canned one of her top executives—on the day bad earnings were announced. In August 2004, when the computer maker reported disappointing earnings for the third quarter, Fiorina called it "unacceptable" and fired three vice presidents from the Customer Solutions Group. This was Fiorina's style. Find a scapegoat, issue the pink slip, problem solved. Returning to private life, she may realize it doesn't quite address the needs of a new economic world.

The Walt Disney Company of the 1990s stands out as the best example of a company whose entire personality seemed to change, almost overnight, for the worse—as a result of an even worse sort of tough-guy leadership—with a similar outcome for the CEO. I never knew the founder, who was reputed to be a shrewd, demanding, and sometimes eccentric businessman as well as a creative genius. But during my years at Y&R, which coincided with the Michael Eisner era, we did business with Disney on and off, working for them on movies, on various theme park assignments, and other projects. The company is filled with thousands upon thousands of wonderful people, dedicated, hard-working, and smart. I always respected the management duo of Michael Eisner and Frank Wells, which ran the company during the early years of my involvement. In particular, I got to know Wells, and I deeply admired his business skills as well as his fairness and integrity. In the beginning, it was a great company to have as a client.

However, in April 1994, the sixty-two-year-old Wells died in a helicopter crash on a skiing trip. After that, Disney became much more aggressive with its suppliers, driving down prices, demanding concessions, and constantly changing requirements. At Y&R, evenhanded negotiations were replaced by a winner-take-all stance, and Disney was determined always to win, by any means. Even after agreeing to certain conditions in a deal, Disney seemed unwilling to abide by them. It got so bad that one way or another, in almost every case, its management would try to weasel out of its obligations with us—written or oral—about financial payments, scope of projects, and so on. It became intolerable.

Finally, I sent word to all our subsidiaries around the world that we'd no longer do business with Disney because its culture had deteriorated so badly. It's the only large company I've ever had to take such a step with. In a sense, it was both a practical and a values-based decision. We could have continued to put up with the abuse to make some money from the account, but if we had, I would have been a partner in that abuse—allowing our people to suffer under Disney's tactics, simply to make money. By cutting our ties with Disney, Y&R was going to take a hit to the top line, and maybe the bottom line as well, but I didn't believe it was right to ask my people to put up with it any longer. It would have been too demoralizing. It also reflected badly on Y&R's own culture—judging our people by the company they chose to keep.

Eisner may not have *ordered* this cultural change, but the shift inevitably followed from his character and his style of leadership. Eisner, for example, hired a man who was ostensibly his best friend, superagent Michael Ovitz, and then apparently turned on him and betrayed him almost immediately. A November 23, 2004, article in the *Wall Street Journal* talks about this episode: "Time and again in the Ovitz case, including Mr. Eisner's own account, [the story] illustrates how he operated with little regard to conventional rules of corporate play. He allowed rivalries to fester until they became irreparable, lied publically when it was convenient, and once hatched a plot with a director to report details of a private conversation with Mr. Ovitz."

A take-no-prisoners arrogance had become the Disney way. As James Stewart puts it so well in *DisneyWar* (2005), "His management failures include . . . a frequent mistrust of subordinates, impulsive and uncritical judgments, his pitting of one executive against another, his disrespect for any hierarchy of authority other than his own, his encouragement of a culture of spying and back-channeling, his frequent failure to acknowledge the achievements of others." I can't imagine this sort of leadership as a good way to attract or keep the best talent in any industry, let alone the creative fields Disney specializes in. And nothing could be more at odds with the Disney brand image. Because Disney is still considered one of the best at what it does, maybe the leadership believed it could treat people any way it liked. But why create an atmosphere where some people who work for you are secretly rooting for your departure? Depart he has, with a new CEO appointed by the board in the spring of 2005.

The New Rules

Why have tough guys thrived down through history? Because it worked. It was effective and often necessary. In the military, that kind of leadership has been the rule, and in business it dates back at least to the early part of the Industrial Revolution where human beings were merely the substitutes for what machines do today. Their tasks were repetitive, mechanistic, and mind-numbing. Even in the twentieth century, they became extensions of the machine, with robotic tasks. The few were creative thinkers; the rest simply did what they were told.

Almost half a century ago, Douglas MacGregor, in his oft-cited book *The Human Side of Enterprise*, divided managers into two types who managed based on opposite views of human nature. Theory X, as he described it, held that human beings were fundamentally lazy, unmotivated, and would shirk work at any opportunity. This view justified tough-guy leadership: motivation through force, enticement, fear, and rewards. Theory Y held that people were naturally self-motivated, creative, productive, and enjoyed work—in the right environment. People could be motivated with respect and given the freedom to achieve in the jobs with minimal supervision, given the right work environment.

Theory Y, like free enterprise, has won the battle at last. The excess supply world has made it the only view of human nature that works.

Here's the logic of my argument. The customer rules everything now because in an excess supply world with an ever-greater number of choices and relative sameness of product offerings, the consumer is in a position to choose products and dictate to the providers. The relationship between product and customer has been redefined as brand identity, and the prevailing brand will create this intimacy and trust with customers as well as satisfy functional needs. So a relationship of trust and loyalty with customers will become all-important, which requires respect for, and from, employees. If the culture within a company isn't built on trust and honesty and fairness, customers will encounter workers who just don't care. Loyalty erodes and disappears.

More and more employees interface with customers and those encounters govern, with ever greater significance, how the customer feels about the brand. Employees are no longer robots. They become brand representatives to the consumer, deepening the relationship. Even the back room staffers have their impact on the consumer by what they do themselves and by how they influence the quality of life for the people on the front line. They're all players in the same game. They help invent and create extensions of the meaning of the brand to the consumer. Tales were once told of how Nordstrom employees would go out of their way to provide service to their clients, returning lost items to hotels in the middle of the night, taking charge of providing merchandise to customers when it wasn't available in a particular store. Ritz-Carlton is another exemplary company. In Chicago, recently, I used a limo service to get from the airport to Ritz-Carlton. When I arrived off Michigan Avenue, a reception clerk greeted me and handed me my key. He must have gotten a call from the driver that we were getting close. "You can sign at the desk whenever you like. Your luggage will follow." This is exactly the kind of dedication and focus on the customer all companies need, and the corporate leader must lead the charge in this direction, often by personal example.

Enlightened leaders, then, will be defined by a new set of qualities. They must develop cultural values in addition to business goals and objectives. They must be able to communicate and convince all the critical constituencies: employees, shareholders, financial community, customers, consumers, vendors, and so on. Talking the talk is not enough. Fierce dedication to quality and customer satisfaction is *learned* behavior, and in an organization the learning flows from the top down. We are conditioned from childhood to imitate those we admire: parents, teachers, and idols in any realm of experience. It's true in sports, in the military, in academia, and in business: one of the significant ways we learn to behave is by watching how our role models behave. Enlightened leaders must embody the mission in both personal and corporate values.

Since creativity—the continual process of inventing new, customized solutions to customer needs—is now the pivotal ingredient for success, enlightened leaders must set high aspirations and demand creative excellence from everyone. Enlightened leaders know how to be demanding but always fair. If the goals are reasonable and the demands fair, the goals can be set very high.

The authors of *Creativity in Business* describe the conditions required to come up with new ideas, new products, and new approaches to the market. It happens in an atmosphere where a strong-willed effort to succeed is paired with intuition, joy, and compassion. The first half of that sentence—strong-willed effort— is familiar to anyone who has ever worked in the private sector. It's the nose-to-the-grindstone part. The second half contains, more or less, three dirty words to anyone who, until recently, has tried to make a quarterly number. Intuition? Joy? Compassion? One can see the stock analysts grow pale and lower their heads in shame. And what do the authors say, in this environment, a team needs to do when faced with the need to innovate?

Quit striving and simply begin by doing what is easy and effortless, applying yourself to the task—do something, don't just sit there. It's reminiscent of Hemingway's rule of always leaving unwritten at least a sentence he knew he was going to write at the end of the day, so that the gears would already be revolving in the morning. Maintain a spirit of inquiry and acknowledge that you don't know in advance how things will turn out. Pay attention to everything, apply yourself with great resolve, but give yourself time to relax and let the process go underground—stories of great insights invariably follow a pattern of intense effort, relaxation, and a sudden realization at the least likely moment. Ask dumb questions and be willing to fail again and again, but don't give up.

These guidelines are significant, not because they are the only way to come up with innovative ideas, but because they are, by and large, inconsistent with the sort of behavior tough-guy leadership would encourage.

Not *everything* has changed, though. The leader must be decisive without ducking tough calls, listening, learning, and acting but always willing to explain decisions so that mission is consistent with values. Enlightened leaders subscribe to the management style of *we*. The "I" word loses power, meaning, impact. The new world is ever more about cooperation and teamwork. Company leadership must reflect that attitude. The one at the top must make sure the decisions are made, ideally by consensus, but ultimately they have to be made, and made quickly, and often *against* the consensus. Top leaders can't duck the tough, unpopular calls. They must have a bias for action.

Finally, enlightened leaders must be, foremost, the cheerleaders, advocates, and supporters of the consumer, the customer's interest. That is the true north toward which the organization's compass always points. As always, you have to set goals, make decisions, hold people accountable, and fire those who don't perform: but how you do it is the key. Enlightened leaders operate much like Olympic figure skaters, who win points for technical merit and competence and also for stylistic execution. To sustain success over the long term, they must perform at the highest level in both ways: no matter how good you may be on competence, that's only one part of the final report card. It's style that shapes the soul of how a company operates. You must be and act as a good person who genuinely recognizes the intrinsic value of the human beings who serve you—a leader who genuinely cares about every single worker—leading with respect for those who serve the organization.

Baked Fresh Daily

In 1996, Young & Rubicam pitched Dell with a new slogan: Baked Fresh Daily. I was disappointed that it didn't win us the account, because I had enormous respect for Michael Dell and the organization he created. It stands among only a few others as close to the perfect prototype of a company designed, down to the last detail, for success in the new world of excess supply.

The extraordinary act of creativity that reverberates through everything Dell does from day to day was in the creation of the business model itself. It eliminated the gap between customer and product, and it put as much creativity into the hands of the buyer as the producer. The consumer skips wholesale and retail and steps right up to the assembly line, in a virtual way: designing the product before it gets built. All of this is backed up by superior service, operational excellence, a voracious appetite for gathering and analyzing data about customer desires and behavior, and consistently low prices. Dell is the quintessential example of productivity in the new economy: delivering a superior product for less money.

The story is well known how Michael Dell's passion for computers in college led him to drop out of school and build a radically new kind of business. As a student with a desire to buy a good computer—and predicting there would be many more like himself with the same desire—he saw the only channel filled with retailers who marked up the machines by 30 percent without knowing a thing about them and who offered almost no service. The unknowing buyer was being milked by an unknowledgeable seller. It was a simple proposition: sell computers he would upgrade himself directly to his own customers, adding knowledge and service to the equation and charging much less for the product. He started in his dorm room, moved his business into a condo, then into a business center, and then kept having to move into new quarters, more than twice as big, every few months.

As he went along, with such close contact with customers, he learned to build a database about them, what they bought, why they bought it, and what they would buy in the future. But the crucial lesson he learned was to ask each of the customers what they wanted *before* he built their computers. As he wrote in *Direct from Dell:* "And with every new customer, we gathered more information about their product and service requirements. It was the perfect closed loop." Dell created such a close relationship with customers that it would consult with them before throwing itself into a new line of business or a new system for service and support. Customers weren't simply flattered. They realized the company wanted to build a relationship for life with them, and not just another sale.

It wasn't a steady, untroubled rise. From 1987 through 1993, the company struggled with growing pains, venturing into uncharted product territories, stepping into the traditional retail channels and then pulling out, and finding that it had to reverse itself and learn quickly from its mistakes. At the end of the struggle, it acquired many of the old, traditional competencies: a massive, organizational focus on four thousand different measurements of productivity and success, numbers it learned to crunch in every possible way. It broke itself down into business units focused not on products but on market segments—each with its own P&L—defined by customer behavior rather than traditional demographics. It became, in other words, a corporation with a strategic thrust growing out of a focus on the customer—a not-unfamiliar organization structure for the 1990s. It achieved operational excellence, and it anticipated key shifts in the market, primarily with its move into the server business.

What also emerged from this period of trial was enlightened leadership: expressed primarily in a system of matrix management, a willingness to share power at the top. Michael Dell brought on board two people who helped him run the entire corporation: Mort Topfer from Motorola, and Kevin Rollins from Bain & Company. With overlapping accountability, the CEO worked with his two partners to focus the entire company around segmented markets, determined by customer needs and behavior. During this period, emerging from its troubles, Dell laid the final cornerstone of its phenomenal success by announcing its Web site: www.dell.com. In 1996, it began selling desktops and servers over the Internet, becoming a business model perfectly suited to the age of excess supply. The closed feedback loop of information became a high-bandwidth circuit now, enabling the company to test ideas, measure them, and give them a thumbs up or down in the course of an hour—tests and shifts that would have taken months to deploy in the pre-Internet age.

Since he began, Michael Dell has been eager to share power and credit for his achievements. He has been known for "management by walking around"—the old Tom Peters principle of excellence—talking to people at all levels, soliciting genuine comments and ideas on how to improve. The humility this implies carries throughout everything the leadership team does. Everyone in the company essentially answers to everyone else they work with. Everyone, from Dell and Rollins on down—Topfer retired three years ago—is subject to a 360-degree performance appraisal—soliciting input from everyone who works with or for them. The company has also begun a new program called Tell Dell, a less formal twenty-four-question employee survey that ranks how people are doing in their jobs—in this case the two men running the company.

In a recent conversation with me, Kevin Rollins put it into perspective:

> We all know one another's scores. We've developed an open culture of "It's OK not to do well as long as you improve it." Now the whole culture has moved to a new level of sophistication and trust and loyalty. Michael and I have shared both our 360 evaluations and our Tell Dell scores with everyone for a number of years. Including the press.

Honest vulnerability like that sets the tone for a culture of trust and the creativity that follows. What's funny is that you'll never want to use the word *creative* with Kevin Rollins: if you twist his arm, he'll admit his organization is constantly trying to find creative solutions for customers, but he just won't use the word. It smacks of art. Ambiguity. Wiggle room. He wants everyone to know whatever is innovative and new at Dell is about *winning,* and has nothing to do with the loosey-goosey, anything-goes milieu he associates with . . . that word.

> We don't talk about creativity but about winning culture. We want to win and be the best at everything we do. It's excellence. Whenever we get into something, we study what's out there and do the best. Our attitude is, let's totally rewrite the book. Let's put new ideas into this plus some legacy thinking. We spend $600 million dollars on R&D, but we are very disciplined that within the scope of customer need we don't spend on frivolous things. We do it in a very precise way. Our competitors spend far more on R&D and have much inferior financial performance. You take someone like Apple which is very creative but they can't get a payback on that investment. *We* don't use the "creative" word, but it's a fine word.

Without using that word, let's just say it's safe at Dell to try out new ideas and fail, as long as you do it fast. Rollins adds,

> We're open to ideas, and you want people to participate so you keep an entrepreneurial spirit alive. Michael's style is to bring the spirit of keeping everything open. Everybody feels he or she is rewarded and encouraged to develop good ideas. There's a certain benevolent chaos or, mischievous is not the right word, but there's a spirit of independence: *I run my own business.* When we evaluate all the ideas, we get quickly to *The answer is A, we're all going in this*

direction. We have a strong bias for action. That's the command-and-control side of it. How long does the talking last? Not very long. People have to be crisp and data driven and they get it out quickly. Michael wants to discuss more and I want to discuss less.

Lead ership drives urgently toward the point of a decision, but it doesn't force what's going to happen. In many instances, Rollins said, he and Dell allow their team to take them in a direction they hadn't anticipated.

In one instance, Michael and I had firm ideas on human resources and hiring and training. Our leadership team told us they didn't like what we had planned. They said they had some better ideas. We opened discussions on HR policy, hiring policy, compensation, many things to the whole team: the top fifteen or sixteen people. We opened those discussions *broadly*. And we learned. We found they had great ideas, and our ideas didn't encompass all the options. After that, the buy-in was far better. We use that model now for almost everything. IT [information technology] spending is a big one. We have great participation and dialog across the organization. But we don't belabor it. We get to, *The answer is* X, *we've all talked, now we're going*.

That tension, that *creative* tension—sorry Kevin—between the idea-generating organization and the bias for action from the top is part of the reason Dell has become one of the most successful companies in history, and one of the most trusted brands ever to emerge. Alas, their future, like their past, won't always be smooth. Their commitment to customer intimacy, to superior customer service, will be tested. If Dell service isn't as easy to access as it used to be, or if scripted outsourced service technicians sometimes struggle with the language barrier, it may be a warning sign that Dell's relationship with customers needs fine-tuning. Yet what matters is how Michael, Kevin, and their organization respond to the next chapter of challenges. I'm betting—literally, as a shareholder—that they will rise to the challenge, and with an inborn will to win and prepare, they will succeed.

The Confident Smile

The most ubiquitous product in the world, more widespread than even Coca-Cola, is Colgate toothpaste. It operates in hundreds of countries. It continues to bring clean, white teeth and fresh mouths everywhere because of the leadership of Reuben Mark. He's one of today's most enduring executive leaders, chairman of Colgate-Palmolive since 1986—and a man with a confident smile all his own. Reuben has delivered shareholder value with consistency and attracted and kept top people, all while withstanding the onslaughts of corporate raiders eager to take over his company on terms that could easily have enriched him at the expense of his shareholders. Behind one of the longest records of quarter-on-quarter increases, lasting more than twenty years, is the kind of quiet but steely leadership of this wonderful man.

Sometimes enlightened leadership takes you by surprise. For a long time, you think you're dealing with an old-school type, until you finally discover the true character of the person in charge. When we won the Colgate account in the 1980s, we got more than we bargained for. They didn't simply want us to do what we'd been doing for so many years for all our clients. They wanted us to take it all to a completely new level, with service integrated for their needs in ways we'd never dreamed. We didn't willingly enter this new frontier. Some of our most essential and rewarding innovations were driven by demanding clients, asking us for more than we'd ever before offered.

Reuben Mark and the top team at Colgate met with us to establish their expectations. What they told us went beyond *our* expectations in a startling way. He didn't want campaigns, slogans, pieces and parts of a communication strategy. He wanted comprehensive solutions that drew upon our talent everywhere and required us to act not simply as marketing consultants but as partners in shaping the company's entire strategic vision.

"We want you to integrate what you do for us around the globe," Reuben said. "You've got 460 offices in eighty countries. It shouldn't be too much to ask that people in all those offices feel they are part of a team devoted to Colgate."

This was a stunning request. It seemed daunting to try to pull together such a disparate array of resources. Mark went into greater detail. He wanted us to be able to translate and transfer brilliant marketing ideas and campaigns across markets. It might be as obvious as taking a slogan that worked in Thailand and deploying it in cultures where it was appropriate. We needed to be able to coordinate across various global markets, leverage good ideas from one market in others, and take advantage of economies of scale. He wanted us to be able to experiment with new initiatives where products were ripe for improvement and then apply the results in various other places. You have to know a lot about customers and markets to do this, but—and this is the tough part—you have to be able to align your entire organization to communicate with one another, along with the required systems, and they will coordinate these efforts on a global basis. I credit Reuben Mark and Colgate, along with Bill Shanahan and the top teams around them, for pushing Y&R hard to develop this capability and execute it around the world. Bill Shanahan is to Reuben Mark as Rollins is to Michael Dell.

As chairman of Colgate-Palmolive, Reuben is tough as nails, but there is a fairness and integrity at the heart of that toughness. He never accepts anything but superlative work and can make you feel, at times, as if he doesn't appreciate you at all—but it's actually a sign of his immense faith in your ability to shine. His attitude is fair: if *he* is the problem, he is more than willing to take responsibility and fix it. But if you are the problem, which can be the case, more often than not, he won't rest until you've fixed it.

In my work with him, there were times when, because of his toughness, I wondered if Reuben really recognized the kind of value we were generating for his company—and wondered, as well, if he wasn't just a tough guy interested in results nobody could be asked to achieve. All my doubts were erased when I went on a road show to garner support for our first issue of stock, and I discovered that Reuben had spoken with many of the same analysts on his Colgate rounds before we arrived, and when they asked about Y&R he praised us in ways it would seem less than humble to repeat in print. Those few words from him made our lives immeasurably better and simpler at that critical juncture. In a way, it wasn't until then that I fully realized what an honorable leader he was, the fairness and honesty at the heart of that tough, hard-to-please exterior.

What makes him an extraordinary leader? First, he personally embodies all the skills and competence required to succeed in this competitive business. As a career Colgate employee, he has lived in every continent of the world. He has performed most of the tasks in the company himself, rising from one job to another. He's an inspirational contributor and problem solver himself. Therefore, he represents the epitome of the man who walks the walk. However, he is also one of the most successful delegators, allowing other people the freedom to lead, to contribute, to invent, while at the same time knowing just when to be involved in the critical decisions. He's not an absentee CEO but a man who empowers his people and yet holds them accountable and tracks their performance in ways that are remarkable both for their effectiveness and for the way they enhance and preserve people's sense of autonomy and accountability. Of the major clients of Y&R, Reuben Mark was one of the most demanding the agency ever had. He set painfully high standards—he

always let you know in very specific ways exactly what he wanted—
and was personally involved in the measurement of the agency's
performance on a regular basis. However, his ability to push for the
highest level of performance and get the most value from the
agency was guided by his ability to be absolutely fair. He was a man
of his word and never failed to live up to his promises.

Craig Middleton, a one-time vice chairman of Y&R, who has
worked with Reuben for a couple of decades, put it best when he
told me:

> They expect us to behave as partners and not suppliers. It's a burden
> and a privilege. We feel a deep responsibility because they have
> treated us so fairly. I have never cared more for a piece of advertising
> than I do with Colgate. As a leader, he's an artist. He has meetings
> with his people daily, weekly, annually, and he comes very well pre-
> pared. Everyone does. He simply asks questions. He doesn't com-
> mand. He will go to individual people and ask their opinion on what
> they're working on, where Colgate is making it easier for them and
> where Colgate is falling short, and he follows up. At that same time
> as he's offering his support, he's expecting that person to say the
> things he wants to hear: to report on results. All things are in
> the open. You're on view. It's a motivating meeting because you
> know it's coming up, you know you have to be prepared with results,
> therefore you have to get those results before the meeting. You don't
> want to be tongue-tied. You don't want to let him down.

He added, "I'm soon to be sixty-two. You get to the point where
you say you've probably seen it all. Working with these guys I've
relearned all my management techniques. I've relearned everything."

Reuben Mark is a stickler, a man who demands that whenever
Colgate is involved and the Colgate brand is presented, the
communication needs to be uncompromisingly fair, honest, and
true. At no time does his culture allow shortcuts or working close

to the line of honesty and integrity. It's interesting to note that, to my knowledge, Colgate has almost never been written up by the extraordinarily tough press as a company in trouble with regulators or the law, one of the few multinationals that successfully manages its business with total integrity.

Reuben Mark does, however, have a flaw. Don't ever try to compliment him. He'll cut you off. He'll get uncomfortable. He'll refuse to take credit for anything. He is, in short, about as enlightened as a leader can get.

The Authentic Leader

In 1989, when Bill George joined as its president and COO—quickly becoming CEO—Medtronic, now the world's leading medical technology company, had $755 million in sales and four thousand employees. When he retired in 2001, he'd grown Medtronic into a $5.5 billion giant with twenty-six thousand workers. For five years, the company was voted one of *Fortune* magazine's best companies to work for in an annual survey of ten thousand corporate executives nationwide. Shareholders were just as delighted by George's leadership: Medtronic's market cap rose from $1.1 billion to $60 billion, a compound return of 35 percent a year.

There is virtually no better example of enlightened leadership than Bill George. You can see a direct link between his value-driven guidance and the company's long history of innovation. Under his leadership, his people invented treatments for incurable diseases, improving the lives of customers in ways unimaginable without Medtronic technology.

The irony is that George resisted Medtronic for a decade—its leaders invited him to join the company no less than four times starting in 1978, and three times he turned down the offers. He felt the company was too small for the big things he wanted to do in life. Before he could recognize the opportunity it offered him, he needed to change as a person. His entire orientation as a leader had to undergo a radical shift—in a sense, he had to realize who he really *was* before he could see his true path as a businessman.

From his childhood, George was intensely idealistic, but—as he shows in his book *Authentic Leadership*—his altruism was working hand in hand with fierce, egocentric ambition. When he was ten years old, he watched as his father was driven out of business by General Motors, notorious for demanding prices so low that vendors often went bankrupt by trying to supply the automotive giant. His father was president of a small automobile parts company in Grand Rapids, and GM kept squeezing until his father was forced to sell out. At some level, George resolved he wanted to be in control of that kind of power in his life, and use it for good.

It didn't come easy to him. While he was in college, he lost seven elections in his fraternity, until his brothers told him he was too self-centered to win votes. He needed to pay more attention to others. He did, and it changed everything for him, but his egocentric orientation only got stronger: his success in "paying attention to others" was a way of getting ahead.

At Litton Industries, the big conglomerate where he was fast-tracked after working at the Harvard Business School and the Pentagon, he was put in charge of its microwave oven business when he was only twenty-seven. His dreams seemed to be coming true when a trade magazine did a cover story on him: "Litton's George changes the way America cooks." But after fifty-five consecutive quarters of earnings growth, he learned the numbers had been engineered by dipping into reserves that bolstered profits in lean times. People there would do anything to make the numbers. He left, and, at Honeywell, found himself again and again butting up against truths about himself he didn't want to see.

He rose to be in charge of eighteen thousand employees, on his way to becoming CEO, the dream of his youth. When a little company in Minneapolis called, offering him the No. 2 job, he dismissed it, having never heard of Medtronic. It was beneath his ambitions, his ego, his dream. Medtronic called two more times. Twice more: *no*.

At Honeywell, he was known as the one who could come in and fix one bad division after another. He'd do what he was asked to do and then move on. But something was wrong. He was miserable.

I wanted to be CEO badly, but I no longer knew why. Driving home one afternoon it hit me: Honeywell was changing me more than I was changing Honeywell. I wasn't building anything; I wasn't creating anything. Sure, I was leading, but I no longer knew where my leading was leading to. I realized that I too was becoming imprisoned by the Game. I called Medtronic and asked if the job was still available. It was, and this was the luckiest break I ever got. It was during that long, agonizing process that I discovered the voice I should listen to. In business school we watched the 1962 film *The Loneliness of the Long-Distance Runner*, yet only recently have I come to relate to the film's protagonist. During his solitary cross-country runs through the woods, he's accompanied only by voices and images from his troubled past. In the CEO's case, those voices are very real: "Manage for the short run," they say. "Take the shortcut. Beware the short-sellers." The test of leadership is ignoring those outside voices and learning to hear the one deep within. As a CEO, your attention ultimately has to be on the long run—and that is, of necessity, a lonely run. The voices clamoring for your attention will be many. Your job is to find your own.

Great leaders, George says in his book, must go through a crucible, an experience that tests their endurance, resolve, and faith. Often the great leader is the one who stays and fights when he faces an overwhelming challenge, rather than move to another company. In George's case, it meant leaving a path that seemed to offer him everything he wanted.

It finally dawned on me that I was so caught up in my drive to run a major corporation that I was in danger of losing my soul. I remembered the vision I'd had of myself as a teen: leading a mission-driven, values-centered corporation where I was passionate about the company's products and the opportunity to serve others. What better place to do it than Medtronic?

It was a magic move. Yet almost immediately after he started with the company, he faced a decision that forced him to listen to his inner voice and no other. His colleagues had worked out a strategy to settle a major patent lawsuit against Siemens: it would give Siemens the use of a patent without paying royalties to Medtronic, an alliance which might create future opportunities for both companies. It didn't feel right to him. He stood alone against the group, a stance that made him immediately unpopular with nearly everyone he had to lead. But his stubborn adherence to his instincts allowed his company eventually to settle with Siemens for more than $400 million, which, at the time, was the second-largest settlement in history.

Standing alone on this issue was only half the test of his character. Over the years, as those royalties came in, the true test emerged. Again, he was under pressure from those around him, this time to apply the royalties to the bottom line. The real measure of George's enlightened leadership was his insistence on *not* counting these royalties as profits. The temptation, and the encouragement from everyone else, to simply account the royalties as earnings must have been nearly overwhelming. With a goal of 15 percent growth every year, a recurring trial by fire if there ever was one, it would have been so easy to please Wall Street by inflating the numbers this way. Instead, George insisted the company reinvest the royalties in a series of new ventures under the banner of a program called Reinventing Medtronic. As part of this campaign, they raised R&D spending from 9 percent to 12 percent of revenues, even though everyone understood that investment wouldn't yield any bottom-line return for five to ten years.

Now, more than a decade later, these investments have generated breakthroughs on multiple fronts, helping to treat heart failure, Parkinson's disease, cerebral palsy, incontinence, atrial fibrillation, and epilepsy. He decided to devote those royalties to the suffering people his company could help: his customers. The customers came first, not the shareholders. And this was the key to his leadership; everything he did grew out of a passion for the company's mission of helping people, and this passion spread throughout the company. Eventually, the shareholders got wealthier—but only as a result of the fulfilled mission.

"I can't imagine telling a worker at Medtronic she needed to make the best pacemaker she could to please Wall Street—or for that matter to please the company's shareholders," George says. "What does my employee care about some fund manager or trader? She doesn't. So what does motivate her? I once asked a Medtronic worker who was making heart valves that very question. 'I'm making these valves to save lives,' she said. 'I'm saving 1,000 lives a year. And if I make one bad valve, someone is going to die.'"

Bill George became a different person at Medtronic. He changed the company, and the company changed him, both for the better. At his Medtronic going-away event a longtime colleague described George as "a leader who would be remembered for his passion and compassion." This employee described the day he had learned his son had terminal cancer and called his CEO to tell him. George immediately drove to the hospital, where they embraced and shared some tears and prayers in the hall outside his son's room.

It took years for him to build this sort of relationship with his people. By nature, he was brusque, assertive, strong-willed—self-centered—all the qualities that kept him from being elected to help run his fraternity in college. A man who might have been mistaken for a tough guy by those who didn't know him better. But he struggled to be open and human with every Medtronic employee. When his own wife, Penny, went through treatment for breast cancer, successfully, he wrote e-mail to all Medtronic employees telling them the good news and thanking them for their support during that difficult time. Hundreds of employees wrote back, thanking him for being so open, sharing their own stories of personal trauma. The answering e-mail continued for several *years*—people never forgot the way he had spoken to them as a friend, an equal. And so they stayed in touch.

In employee surveys, more than three-quarters, and sometimes more than 90 percent, of workers say they are proud to work for Medtronic and that the company's mission is consistent with their values. Its customers are the meaning of what everyone does at Medtronic. Nothing could better express the power of George's enlightened leadership than what he said, himself, in his parting speech to his employees: "Over the past twelve years Medtronic has restored fifteen million people to fuller lives and renewed health."

Bill George is my hero. He is tomorrow's enlightened leader today. And so are Michael Dell, Ken Rollins, Bill Shanahan, Reuben Mark, and many others. And tomorrow—many more will hear that inner voice, heed the right instinct to lead the twenty-first century's creative organization in every single industry. What all of them prove, in different ways, with different styles and products and services, is that being a great leader depends on being a good person. And great leadership focuses itself on creating an organization where people can become not just better workers but better human beings, themselves. When that happens, when people feel they are *at home* in the collaborative environment where they work—a spirit only enlightened leadership can foster—then everyone begins naturally, instinctively, to generate unique creative solutions for customers, the sort of creativity that has become the only differentiating factor in a surplus economy, because it keeps the enlightened spirit of the organization alive. When employees, under this kind of leadership, say, *there's nowhere else I would ever want to work*, customers will begin saying, *there's no one else I'd rather buy from*.

4

COMPETENCY

The Essential Tools

When Kentucky Fried Chicken asked Y&R to pitch for its business, the company was one of the largest accounts in the nation. It was a prize, a plum at a time when we desperately needed a big account. It was a risk to invest all of our resources in a plan to win only one account, at that point, but we decided KFC would be it. There would be no other chances in the foreseeable future. We were going to win this account or die in the process. We put together a big team to work on the presentation: Craig Middleton, Jane Bright, Mike Slasberg, and many others, including John McGarry, one of my closest partners in our success at Y&R, who later became president of Y&R. We prepared like madmen, day and night, living on caffeine, snack foods, pizza, and, of course, KFC, mastering everything we could discover about the chicken business and the fast-food industry.

But that was only the start. We could have written a small encyclopedia about fried chicken, but we weren't happy. It didn't feel as if we were thinking about the company *from the inside*, and I wanted to know KFC inside-out. So John McGarry and I flew to Nashville to talk with Marvin Hopper, a multiple store owner and chairman of the franchisee committee that the company had assembled to help choose an agency.

"We want to learn how to make chicken," I said.

Marvin squinted at me.

"My wife has a cookbook. Would that help?"

"We want to know exactly how *you guys* cook chicken," I said.

"Colonel's recipe is our big secret."

"We don't want the recipe. We just want to learn how to use it," I said.

"You mean have one of your people fry chicken for us?"

"I mean John and I want to fry it for you."

"He's dying to wear an apron," John said, shrugging. "And he isn't even a creative type."

We laughed. A day later, he had everything arranged. He'd gotten us permission to work for three days in one of their toughest stores, a real money-maker. If I wanted to know what it was like to cook Kentucky Fried Chicken, I was going to have to learn how to do it in the real world. It was like getting permission to enter a palace that had always been locked: somehow we'd found the magic words to open the gates. We intended to win this business by becoming the client and by understanding the world through the client's eyes.

We cooked chicken. We did biscuits, coleslaw, fruit pies, and gravy. We counted change. We installed light bulbs. We wiped counters. We swept floors—a skill I'd picked up in Europe. We worked in that place for three days, watching customers, listening to the way employees talked, doing original recipe and extra crispy. I didn't decipher the Colonel's recipe for spices, but I did memorize— in my bones—his recipe for making customers happy.

We came away from this immersion in our prospect's business knowing more about fried chicken than I'd ever expected to learn, as well as developing a deep respect for the people who ran these little franchises: the complexity of the day-to-day challenge was enormous. We acquired the kind of crucial, gritty, face-to-face-with-customers competencies that enabled KFC to execute its much larger strategic vision. Without an understanding of those competencies, we didn't really *know* their business well enough to help them lead it. We learned how crucial it becomes to anticipate when customers will flow through the doors, to time the inventory of cooked food so that you get just a little ahead of the curve: enough to serve the food quickly, but not so early that it sits even a little too long under the heating lamps. You can't keep a chicken breast under one of those lamps more than twenty minutes. Beyond that, you have to throw it out. The consistency of the crust, the moisture in the meat—the delicate consistency that feels and tastes just right—these things are lost if the service isn't timed perfectly.

The sheer physical labor of working only eight hours in one of the stores was astounding. We went home each night with sore muscles. I flopped onto my hotel room bed, absolutely exhausted, without even the energy for conversation over a beer. Finally, armed with the ideas we'd developed through this ordeal, with tons of factual research from consumers and what we considered brilliant creative work, we were ready for our presentation to the KFC group. The committee included the company's chairman, Mike Miles, several other executives, and a group of around eighteen store owners, including Marvin Hopper and Jim Collins, who owned several hundred stores. Our presentation ran eight hours. Four hours in our own offices, and four hours in rented space atop the World Trade Center. It went well. Our creative work was not only excellent but completely focused on real challenges the business faced. But seven and a half hours into our pitch, one of the smaller store owners, Mr. Lambeaux, raised his hand and drawled: "We're impressed by all this thinking. You're welcome to come work for free in my store any time you like."

This got a good laugh.

"But I've got a question for you," he said.

"Shoot," I said.

"You keep talking about how terrific our original recipe is and how we should focus on this recipe in our marketing. Well, you're right. It works. I'm getting hungry just listening to you guys."

Another good laugh. So far, they weren't at our expense.

"So. Since the secret formula is so good, why shouldn't we just take that recipe and use it in our extra-crispy chicken?"

There was total silence in the room. The KFC people recognized the trap, but they kept their game faces. They wanted to see how much we really knew about their business. Most of the people on my team, except for McGarry, were silent because they didn't have a clue how to answer the question. I stood up slowly, letting the drama build a bit. Lambeaux had a straight face. So did I.

"Well, that sounds like a great idea," I said, pausing just a moment to let them think I'd fallen for the gambit, "but it's impossible."

"Oh?" Lambeaux asked. "Why's that?"

"Because the extra-crispy is fried in oil, not pressure-cooked. The key to the original recipe is the pressure cooking. No one's ever done that before. It gives you both the taste and the speed you need. The recipe is important. But the pressure cooking is how you made it work. You put those eleven herbs and spices onto a chicken leg and dunk it in a vat of hot oil, all the flavor will go flying off into the oil."

When Lambeaux grinned at me, I knew we passed a critical hurdle to win the account.

Though hard work and skill had, in a sense, earned us this account—we had learned these traditional, classic competencies, the things that made KFC great, the hard way—it was competence of a different sort from the usual facility with words and images. We'd become *cooks*. We'd become our customer to such a degree that we could look at the world through the eyes of the customer's people. It is that level of competence every business needs to connect creatively with its customers every day. By instinct, we were back then learning a new competency for the new economy that was to come twenty years later.

The world of business has three kinds of competency: the kind you need to do business, any kind of business, the kind you need to do business in your industry, and, finally, the competencies required by the new surplus, global economy. Without mastering the first two sets, you can't begin to tackle the last one. In fact, everything in this book, all the principles—creativity, enlightened leadership, and the principles to come in later chapters, alignment and values—all depend entirely on the mastery of the basic competencies I'm going to describe in this chapter. Competency is the conductor of all the other principles. Executional excellence orchestrates these principles and guides them to peak performance. None of the other principles can operate if you aren't working toward flawless execution—following through, fulfilling expectations, staying true to the words you speak to a customer.

The new economic world demands a new way to sustain success, but the fundamental, basic aptitudes of business endure, and, without mastering them, no organization can hope to learn the new competencies. Without flawless execution, the bond between company and customer weakens and eventually breaks. Executional excellence, like quality, used to be a differentiator, but now it's a baseline requirement to simply stay in the game. I learned much of what I know about the importance of competency by frying chicken.

Know Thy Business

First and foremost, know your business. Again and again, even the most enlightened leadership has to verify results while driving decision making down the organization chart, empowering people with accountability at all levels. You track your company the old way, by the numbers, the metrics of profit and loss. When it was creating a revolutionary new paradigm for how to do business, Dell devised its four thousand numerical measures of performance. As I mentioned in Chapter Three, while Michael Dell has brought creative vision to the process of designing and selling computers, Kevin Rollins—running the company alongside Dell—has instilled in the organization a fanatical commitment to flawless execution. The message implicit in every measure of productivity is this: Let's do it right, and let's not deviate from reliable service, *ever*. He doesn't want any soft edges. It's execute, execute, execute. And that's precisely where Dell's creative approach holds fast to the customer. If you can't follow through in a way that builds trust, it doesn't matter how intimately you know what your customer wants.

As always, you need to hire good people and search tirelessly for colleagues superior to you. Surround yourself with workers whose talents seem to outshine your own. Firing is just as important as hiring. Being an enlightened leader doesn't mean being soft. You have to know when to fire the bad fits and make the tough calls: it's the right thing to do for the person you have to let go. But when you have to make a cut, do it thoughtfully, and understand the psychological impact on the individual and, to whatever degree possible, reach out to help that person in maintaining dignity and finding a better, more suitable opportunity.

Have a strong bias for action. You will find this, again and again, in every successful organization. There's plenty of listening going on, but there's no delay, no stalling—leadership is open to ideas and suggestions and offbeat solutions to intractable problems, but the brainstorming doesn't drag. There are no filibusters in the conference room. People look to leaders to lead, and no matter how much you empower your people, you can't give them the power *not* to move forward. An egg timer belongs on every CEO's desk. Time is one of the few resources that will never become a commodity.

Develop and instill a healthy work ethic everywhere. Reasonable balance will bring greater fulfillment to both your personal life and your business life. But manage your expectations. Tomorrow's extraordinarily competitive landscape will demand serious commitment and sacrifice.

It bears repeating: Know how to read financial statements. Crunch the numbers in the back of your annual report. Measure and track everything you can. It has been said with great validity that tasks not measured will be least likely to succeed. So if it matters, measure it and track it. And hold people accountable for progress.

Listen with renewed effort every day. Listen to your own hunches, which might seem counterintuitive at the time. Some of the best ideas come from directions you least expect. Listen to everyone, all your critical constituencies. It requires practice, a great deal of humility and concentration. But again: don't listen *too* long. Persuade others, once you've made a decision.

Old Competencies Have a New Target

All these enduring competencies, as essential as they are, must be refocused and aimed at a moving target: the consumer. You can have a company that's a perfectly well-oiled machine by internal standards—everything gets done on time, people show up—but it has lost its way in the external world. You need to take all these traditional competencies and turn them ninety degrees, as it were, so that they all face outward. What happened in the seventies, major companies in America and Europe, considered impregnable, began to find their market shares being eroded by foreign competitors, particularly from Japan.

Complacency had taken hold of those leading companies. Success was deemed a given right in perpetuity. They became blind to the changing world. But nothing stays the same. Customers move on. Technology changes. Competitors can find ways to produce better products faster, cheaper. The rate of change is accelerating now at a dizzying pace. High-quality cheap labor from China and India is doing what Japanese competitors did so successfully a quarter century ago. Companies like Xerox, Kodak, Mercedes, BMW, GM, Motorola, and many others faced constant assaults from Japanese ingenuity, the rise of the global economy, now digital technology and a fast-evolving, more discerning consumer with choices greater than at any point in business history.

What saved some of the companies was a dramatic reorientation to the outside. They took their competition seriously. They went back to basics and relearned their fundamental competencies. They found ways to improve both quality and productivity at the same time. And most important, they took the inspiration for the direction of their business from their customers, their consumers. They've rebounded by adapting and learning what their customers want from them, rather than trying to continue to sell what they, as manufacturers, wanted to produce. Henry Ford's early-twentieth-century dictum—"My customers can have any car color they want as long as it's black"—was clearly no longer operative.

The truth of this is illustrated by the recent history at Procter & Gamble. P&G was, for decades, a juggernaut of consumer goods. It got so good at many of the old competencies of brand management that its management didn't realize the economy of excess demand was coming to an end. They knew how to make great, high-quality products with enormous brand recognition through heavy investment in mass-market communication. They moved in, dominating the marketplace for laundry detergent or diapers and saturating that market with huge advertising and promotion budgets. They were so great at it, they took their formula around the world. As a company, P&G started to believe its own press clippings heralding its successes. It went beyond confidence to a kind of institutional arrogance.

But as the 1990s progressed, and as the paradigm shifted from excess demand to excess supply, P&G's business began to erode. Even so, its managers clung to their arrogance and were unwilling to accept that many of their brands were becoming commodities. Consumers, faced with better price choices and increasingly undifferentiated products, were walking away in droves. Sales slowed, profits decreased, innovation stalled, and the stock market lost confidence in the leadership skill sets of the once great P&G machine.

After several changes in leadership, enter A. J. Lafley, who became CEO in 2000. Though Lafley hasn't publicly articulated the dramatic shift from excess demand to excess supply, judging from his actions he does see with clarity the fundamental shift toward the importance of the consumer.

In his few years at the helm, Lafley has completely reversed P&G's decline. When he took over, P&G had missed two quarterly earnings numbers, cutting its stock price in half. Now, the giant's sales and profits are logging double-digit growth and the stock market is once again rewarding P&G with distinctively high PE multiples. Lafley's philosophy is simple: take dead aim at the consumer. The consumer is boss. What Lafley has done is to reorient his company back to the critical old competencies, the basics, but then refocused them on the consumer. He changed the attention of the company from an inside orientation to the consumer's needs. His way of doing this was to teach P&G to recognize the critical importance of two moments of truth: the instant when a consumer chooses which product to pick off the shelf, and the equally important moment when the consumer chooses to *keep using* it.

"I'm a big believer in consumer pull," Lafley told *Advertising Age* in 2004. "We want to be responsive to the marketplace, to consumers, to retailers."

Under Lafley's leadership, the company has invested a lot of power and influence in its Market Development Organizations (MDOs). In the past, those assigned to an MDO felt as if they'd been exiled almost into a staff position. They had sway over media choices, they developed multibrand promotions, but they didn't spearhead advertising or have much say over how an individual brand was managed. Now they have P&L responsibility, with all the prerogatives that go with it. The effect of this shift is to drive decision making down to the level where people at P&G have their fingers on the pulse of much more individualized consumer market segments. That pulse is what governs the activities of the MDO.

It's a way of building grassroots solutions, working up from consumer behavior rather than trying to drive behavior with mass-market communications to serve preexisting notions of what people will buy.

"The objective is to be relevant as part of the consumer's life in a deeper, more accepted way than brands are today," Jim Stengel, P&G's global marketing officer, told *Adweek*. "First, go deep in your understanding of your consumer. Be part of their lives. Market to them in a way they find relevant and acceptable. Think about when and where they are receptive to our brand message, to our brand, and then do your creative work."

It means reaching consumers in ways specific to smaller groups, and in ways that go beyond traditional communications: pushing Charmin as the toilet paper for rest rooms at state fairs; creating *www.pampers.com* as a source of helpful information for young mothers; and making Prilosec, an over-the-counter treatment for acid reflux, a conduit for knowledge about health issues to the consumer through the pharmacist.

As Stengel puts it: "We have an approach, we have principles, and we have a philosophy that begins with the consumer. So you're seeing much more variability in how we go to market. It gets down to mundane things. We're giving a lot of thought to working with our retailers on how quickly can the consumer find what's right? How simple is the architecture of the brand on the shelf? We still aren't making it easy enough. It even comes down to your package and how to read it."

This new strategy led to the extraordinarily savvy acquisition of Gillette early in 2005. It was a bold purchase many times larger than any of the company's previous mergers, and brought into the fold one of the world's greatest consumer goods brands.

New Competencies for a New World

It's all about the customer. Period. So know your customer as well as you know your business. Know your market and how you are going to approach it. That's the new critical basic competency. Then you face the biggest challenge: excess supply, as I noted in Chapter One. You address it by differentiating your brand and making it relevant to your target audience.

In the new excess supply world, commoditization is the powerful equalizer for all businesses. Technological prowess enables competitors to imitate the innovative leader with extraordinary speed and quality. The net result is that consumers are increasingly presented with product offerings that have a similar look and feel. So if commoditization is the great business curse in the new economy, a program for continuous differentiation is the essential cure.

But constant innovation and differentiation requires of business a new mind-set. It begs for a marketing-driven view of doing business—which is the art and science of connecting a product or a company with a consumer or customer. The emerging successful marketing art form in the excess supply world is the concept of a brand. The brand idea implies an enduring relationship with a consumer, contrasted with the transaction orientation of the excess demand era.

A brand is different from a trademark. A brand represents an invisible contract between a product, service, or company and its consumers and customers. The brand assures the customer of consistent quality and superior value through either a functional or emotional benefit, ideally both. In return, the customer will offer the brand a form of loyalty (though not monogamous) and a willingness to pay a somewhat higher price for it. Marketing in this new world represents all the communication and means of persuasion to keep this contract alive and in proper balance.

To most marketers, the critical question becomes, is my brand strong? Will it keep its power if I cut promotional support? Is my brand becoming a commodity based on competitive action?

This isn't guesswork anymore. Marketing is becoming more of a science. In the past, there was virtually no way to measure your success in differentiating yourself other than whether or not sales were rising for your product. Now, that's not a bad measure of success. Some might say it's the only measure that counts. But while I was at the helm, Young & Rubicam invested many years and $70 million in creating an accurate system to predict the life cycle of a brand, giving a company a way to actually foresee future earnings based on current marketing practice. It's called the Brand Asset Valuator (BAV), and it has proven itself as a reliable tool for measuring the most important effort an organization can make now: creating a strong brand in order to connect in a meaningful way with customers.

The system relies on a comprehensive database—the world's biggest—of consumer perceptions, data on twenty-five thousand brands across forty-four countries, compiled over ten years, information collected on a consistent basis throughout more than two hundred extensive surveys. And the BAV program has continued at Y&R long after my retirement from the company. Using this database, the BAV can compare a brand's strength against both its competitors and other leading brands.

The BAV measures a brand's health on four dimensions:

- *Differentiation:* Does the brand stand out among similar brands?
- *Relevance:* Does the consumer consider the brand useful?
- *Esteem:* Does the brand command respect?
- *Knowledge:* How well do consumers understand the brand?

Differentiation drives margins. Relevance governs market penetration. A brand ranked higher on differentiation than on relevance is on the rise and can enjoy growing sales. A brand that ranks higher on relevance than on differentiation is becoming a commodity. The study of a brand that BAV makes possible means understanding the relationship between brands and why people do or don't buy them—getting down into the granular inner workings of that relationship, not simply whether it's strong or weak.

Most market studies measure awareness and perception of a brand, which are simply outcomes of the key factors BAV measures. In a surplus economy, products in a given category, over their life cycle, tend to become more and more alike. The consumer expects that in today's world. So awareness and perception begin to level out across the market: people are almost equally aware of competing brands and have equal regard for all of them. Without differentiation, you aren't on the consumer's radar screen. Finally more sophisticated analysis demonstrated unequivocally that brands with strong differentiation and relevance will produce significantly higher earnings for their companies.

If an organization doesn't choose to use BAV, it must choose some other measure for tracking brand strength and performance. A company can go through many brand managers. But it lives or dies by the brand itself. So understand the brand's health, manage it, strengthen it, and it can continue to produce profits for as long as you keep it healthy and strong.

Get Intimate with Customers

The only way to distinguish a brand and also make it relevant to individual customers is to know them better than any company dreamed of knowing its customers thirty years ago—or even ten years ago. Inevitably, the seller who knows the customer better than a competitor—who has a closer *friendship* with the customer—will win the sale. The seller must serve the individual customer, each individual customer, one at a time, and the only place this used to work was in a village—and a small one at that. Now the globe is quickly becoming that village. The seller can no longer afford to think of individual buyers as part of a nameless, faceless group. The winners in this economy will get to know each employee and each customer as a unique individual. Pleasing customers and employees, building a relationship with them, will soon become the primary determinant of success.

All these factors build a relationship between a company and an individual customer that induces the customer to do what seems to have become obsolete: pay a slightly higher price for something that otherwise would be a low-priced commodity. The company that creates the most personal and intimate understanding of individual customers—and serves them better, based on this intimacy—recreates the lost quality of being special that premium products once embodied. This loyalty isn't just the result of reputation created through brand-image campaigns based on inflated claims; it's built on genuine value, validated by the customer's own experience of satisfaction. It's based on core values—integrity and genuine service—embodied in everything an organization does. You have to have genuine character, genuine quality. Without quality, without the basics, there will be no loyalty. It has to be real. If it isn't, customers will know, and they will switch easily to another brand, usually a lower-priced brand.

Competencies are going to make all this possible. Short term, a greater emphasis on behavior-driven segmentation. Medium to long term, the magic commercial and communication medium of the future will be the Internet.

Behavior-based market segmentation—marketing toward groups of people who share similar behaviors—will make it possible to take full advantage of the Internet. It will move free enterprise steadily away from mass marketing toward smaller groups of consumers—those who behave in similar patterns, and who share similar attitudinal mind-sets toward a brand. The behavior of the consumer is more important than attitude. Over the years, marketers have found that rationally stated consumer attitudes don't consistently determine what people will buy. What's important is how people live their lives, how they behave. The science of research has not yet learned how to measure consumers' true mind-set.

So in the near term, the most effective marketing will use ever more diverse groups of media best able to reach the diverse consumer segments. Rigorous analytics will value each segment, setting spending priorities for it with an eye toward appropriate and desirable return on investment.

It should be noted that the most powerful traditional medium—network television—is destroying itself. The cause is simple. The consumer or viewer does not have a respectable seat at the decision-making table, in terms of content, but has incredible power now to screen out unwanted messages. The networks still operate by the old excess demand mentality, to their detriment. The most important constituency for the networks are the studios who produce suboptimal programming. (Yes, there are some excellent programs—but not enough and not consistently enough. Lower viewership in the face of other entertainment alternatives proves the point.) Second, the networks are driven by the desire to increase revenues and choose to do it at the expense of viewer satisfaction. Since 1998 the amount of nonprogramming minutes on the networks has increased by 40 percent. Is advertising therefore more effective? Watching the plethora of thirty-second television commercial interruptions is becoming easily avoidable—digital video recorders like TiVo, the ease of clicking to other channels, and the mute button are the death of push marketing on television. Finally, from the advertiser's perspective, the clutter has most likely exceeded the normal human capacity to recall brand names, let alone brand messages. The clutter problem for television is exacerbated by too many undifferentiated messages in a dramatically fragmented media landscape that makes it ever more difficult for marketers to build a brand effectively through television. In time, it is hoped that significantly better measurement of television media consumption and related purchasing behavior of viewers will force the industry to constructively address both the programming and clutter issues.

Enter the Internet. It's the taproot of the new business model. It will make possible a level of interactivity never before seen, which will change the way all companies do business. The answer to the economic realities of our time is *relationship marketing*—an entire business model based on a trusting friendship with individual customers. Technology has made this possible, for the first time in history, on a mass scale.

The Internet makes it happen by creating a link between brand and customer that is instantaneous, free, and easy. It is the ultimate medium. It makes possible many of the things that differentiate a brand. It's global, it's all-pervasive, it's interactive, and it's cheap. No other medium today can compete with it. The next five to ten years will see an entrenchment and expansion of the Internet that will make the dot-com boom seem like a mere foreshadowing of what was to come. And this time the boom will be real and enduring—structural, fundamental, and permanent.

But it will depend on four new and crucial developments.

First, as user-friendly as the typical computer interface has become, it isn't nearly intuitive enough. We have the computing capacity now to do this, to build into the process the algorithms that will make surfing the Web seem as easy and intuitive as riding a bicycle.

Second, interactivity is essential—but it has be an interactive experience where the customer and the brand can come to crucial agreements instantly, with immediate results. That means big bandwidth for everyone.

Third, there needs to be a convergence of electronic appliances into friendlier and more familiar devices: television, stereo, computer, video games, movie players, and PDAs.

Fourth, bricks-and-mortar industries need to become clicks-and-mortar businesses—with an Internet presence that supplements and is coordinated with their physical retail presence. They need the added capability of delivering Internet transactions in high volume. Today, most can't. But the wise ones are hard at work in the process of gaining that capability.

As a medium of communication and commerce, the Internet will likely become, or is becoming, the most powerful the world has ever known. It's ubiquitous. It is by far the least costly medium for communication and commerce since business was done with a handshake. E-commerce will explode and become one of the dominant places of business, locally and cross-nationally. Fulfilling the e-commerce promise will be challenging and expensive. The next likely winners in the short term will be traditional bricks-and-mortar companies that realize the huge potential of this new marketplace and extend their brand into this new space. An important part of the Internet play is the power of interactivity, which elevates the brand relationship to a whole new level. The successful outlets are already there for the world to see. And likely they will be the huge winners in the new world, as they already are today: Dell, Amazon, eBay, and FedEx, among others.

Amazon is the supreme example of this. To discern what drives customer satisfaction now, the *New York Times* conducted a relationship marketing survey of major new world companies. Surprisingly, to those conducting the survey, price alone over time did not impress customers. It cited Amazon as one of the few companies that has registered extremely high on the American Customer Satisfaction Index, the definitive benchmark for how much loyalty and trust customers invest in a particular brand. Amazon claims it has earned this rating by closing the loop of information with its customers and individualizing the Web site for every individual who buys from it, based on that buyer's purchase habits. It has listened to customers and molded itself to the needs and behavior each buyer.

Simply put, Amazon has differentiated the way it offers products and services. It initiates and sustains an intimate relationship with individual buyers that keeps them coming back. To win over the long term, Amazon will have to fix its pricing strategy and its business model, and pay closer attention to this book's values chapter in dealing with partners and suppliers.

The Profit Drivers

There's a wonderful story involving one of the finest living business thinkers, Peter Drucker, and a client who came to him for advice about increasing profitability. Supposedly, the client asked Mr. Drucker how to make money, to which the reply came—you don't make money, you make shoes. Apocryphal or not, it's exactly right. Businesses exist to fulfill a customer need. Profit is indeed the critical by-product, but it's not the driving force of the business. Taking care of the customer is. You can't overemphasize this simple point.

Tomorrow's world will have two aspects to generating profit. The first and increasingly more important is using marketing to increase profitable revenue. The qualifier to revenue growth is critical. There are ways to drive revenues that will decrease the rate of profit for a business. That's very unhealthy, even as a short-term way to penetrate new markets, and in most cases must be avoided at all costs. Embedded in every page of this book is the implicit admonition to generate *profitable* revenue—failing to heed this imperative was one of the principal causes of the dot-com crash. The new context of an excess supply economy is the starting point. The consumer focus, the brand concept, new one-on-one marketing is the contemporary way to drive that revenue. And what gives it power is *differentiation*. It needs to be pointed out that differentiation must first be engineered in the product or services. Enlightened marketing rarely can sustain the perception of differentiation if the product isn't really different. The best, safest, and most reliable path to differentiation is creative product and service innovation. Not once in a while, but a constant program of relevant differentiation. The more visible, palpable, and demonstrable the better. If you want to bet long on the future of a business, bet on a company with a proven understanding of this need and a track record of bringing these relevant differentiations to market, again and again. The fact that Colgate toothpaste is still the leading toothpaste product in the world is proof of just this kind of corporate commitment and competence. And the company has done this over the years even though P&G and Unilever are many, many times the size of Colgate.

In a few product categories highly perceived product differences are hard to achieve, and marketing must do the heavy lifting. These tend to be higher-involvement products where the category benefits have been preempted and protected by a brand over time. Coke, McDonald's, Budweiser are examples. Certainly Marlboro was one in its day. But this is a mightily difficult, challenging task for both the advertiser and the advertising agency. So yes, emotional differentiation can work; in a few instances it's the only solution, but it's a challenging and fragile undertaking. So whenever you can, go to any length to engineer the product differences and use all forms of communication to drive the relationship marketing effort with the consumer based on this real point of difference. Creativity and innovation in product and in communication is the way to the future.

In the excess demand world, it used to be that profit was a simple by-product of sales increases that were not particularly hard to get. In the fiercely competitive world of excess supply, where share battles are the only way to grow, extracting profits from ever-decreasing margins and minimal growth is becoming a critical art and science in its own right. But there is an absolutely critical guideline on how to get profits from the cost side of the business. Businesses must extract cost-side profit from inefficiency and waste and not at the expense of customer benefits or customer satisfaction. That's the iron rule. Violate it and you lose. Sooner or later, cheating your customer will catch up to you and destroy you. So don't do it.

Improved productivity, cutting out waste and inefficiency, is an eternal task. After the dot-com debacle, when the market sank and the economy seemed to stall, help desks and service functions everywhere began to suffer. Companies began to cut back in precisely the worst possible areas: where they interfaced with customers after the sale, where they built and sustained relationships that were the heart of their future. They were still operating with an excess demand mentality. To cut costs in a way that doesn't impair customer relationships requires measurements, creativity, inventiveness, commitment, and persistence. Measurement again is critical because only when a process can be broken down and carefully measured and analyzed can progress be achieved.

Cutting costs the right way is familiar territory for anyone involved in a program of continuous improvement out of the Total Quality movement. When I visited Ford's European headquarters in Cologne, Germany, I arrived dog tired after two days of continuous travel. The people who greeted me told me, to my great relief, that the meeting we'd scheduled for eight the next morning had been pushed back to nine. But then they said they'd filled that wonderful vacuum in my schedule with a plant tour at 7 A.M. I wanted to die, but said, of course, "What a terrific idea!" The next morning, I met two plant managers. One of them, Hans, said: "We'd like to talk to you about what's going on in this plant and how we've improved productivity the last two years by 38 percent." Coffee wasn't needed, after that. I was wide awake when I heard that percentage. But, a little too quickly, I said, "A lot of robotics, huh." Yes, some. "That accounts for about five percentage points," Hans said. What else?

"Well, we have this process here. Every day," he said, "the two of us meet with the six people who report directly to us, and they talk about the problems at the factory floor and all the issues that came up from the day before. Then we make a plan of action for the coming day. Those six people meet with twelve they supervise, and they meet with twelve, and it cascades down. Every day. They spend time every morning and every afternoon trying to figure out what went right and what went wrong. They go home and the two of us meet the next morning and say this is the response to what happened yesterday, and this is what we're doing today."

It was a fascinating way of making productivity a science, a process of tiny, incremental improvements that accumulate over time into big savings. The philosophy they discovered is embedded in the process: break down everything into a million parts, measure each part, analyze the measure, calibrate the process in whatever way you can, and then keep doing it again and again, until it can't get any better.

There is no business today that should not aggressively pursue this effort. But always observe the golden rule. Don't cut anything that strengthens customer loyalty. Never, never cut a customer benefit or satisfaction. Any other avenue is fair game.

Manage for Success

Given all of the new competencies required to interact with the world—out there—you might think the old competencies would be enough *inside* the building. But as much as the old skills are required, they are not enough. A leader can't manage for productive creativity without inspiring confidence.

First, this means creating a strategic intent and making it the foundation of everything an organization does. It's a dynamic, organic vision statement of what the business is about. By identifying the differentiating promises that make a brand unique and relevant to customers, you can build around it a vision of how the company is meaningful to those customers. (In Chapter Five I discuss the Johnson & Johnson Credo, which represents perhaps the most enduring and productive mission statement ever articulated.) The vision statement should be simple, relevant over time, and communicated to and totally embraced by key members of the organization's management group, if not the entire company. It's about the customer, not the company. Bill George of Medtronics created the best example of this: every employee understood and believed in the company's mission of helping people regain their health, and so his company was aligned toward the customer.

With a strategic intent firmly in place, confidence builds. Recently, a number of books have come out about how to nurture organizational confidence. Jonathan Tisch, CEO of Loews Hotels, suggests that successful partnerships are what drive confidence: as long as they are planned and move toward a goal that benefits everyone in the partnership. Rosabeth Moss Kanter, former editor of *Harvard Business Review*, agrees that confidence will gain momentum only when a leader allows and requires people to collaborate, innovate, and keep their word. The way in which leadership inspires and sustains confidence matters less than the simple recognition that without it, you can't succeed. Building confidence is the best way to inspire innovation. Accept responsibility for becoming the student of the creative process and learning how to manage creativity, as discussed in "The Creative Cauldron" section in Chapter Two, but realize that confidence is one of the strongest supporters of a creative process. Show your people you believe in them and they will believe in your mission.

While it may seem like a peripheral element of managing for a new kind of economy, leadership must now take seriously the requirements of parenthood for its employees. Because most households now have two working parents, companies must learn how to manage the situation of new parents intelligently. If we want to capture the creative energy of our people, we must understand that the parenthood issue is a major logistical hurdle for them. Whoever will be the main caretaker of the new children must be managed in a positive and realistic way to provide guidance for the family without disrupting both organizational and functional needs of the enterprise. Innovative ways of handling the challenge include working from home, company day-care facilities, flextime, and leaves of absence: any of these can help turn a potentially disruptive situation into a way of building an even stronger relationship with workers. But the most important competence is to recognize the issue and be willing to deal with it constructively.

Most of all, with the rapid state of change in the marketplace, in technology, in the fluid structure of organizations, leadership needs to realize it can never stop learning. It takes a beginner's mind, even after thirty years of experience. It's the opposite of being a know-it-all. Rollo May, in *The Courage to Create*, talks about the persistent and essential self-doubt behind all genuine conviction. A leader who has no doubts is a fanatic. A leader whose convictions are strong despite doubts is humble, willing to learn and listen, but with a strong bias for action and an enormous self-assurance that survives even the direst crisis. New techniques will evolve, new tools will arrive—new competitors will be born—and the consumer is always in a state of flux. What passes as effective knowledge this month needs an update weeks or months later. Never assume you know it all. It's as if an MBA isn't an end or achievement but simply admits you into the school of continued learning called a career in business. It's only the start.

We Are the World

Finally, a new, essential competency for business leaders has become a form of diplomacy and statesmanship. The global economy requires a global skill set—business is becoming the ambassador of a way of life, a way of working, in cultures that may not entirely trust what a company wants to do within their borders. Free enterprise has become *the* primary influence over the daily lives of people throughout the developed world. As global companies move into the underdeveloped world, these organizations need to connect with the beliefs and hopes of several billion young people who now see little of relevance to their lives in the developed world. We, the business leaders of the free world—be it America, Europe, or anywhere else—need to show them how and why we're offering them a better future. We need to help give them the tools to connect with us and gain our assistance, if and when they are ready for it.

The same can be said about developed world governments. Simply talking and walking tougher around the globe, while it may be necessary when we are in a situation of clear and present danger, will not eliminate the threat posed by the distrust we face around the world. We can't contain the threat and get back to business as usual. We must change the world by closing the chasm between the developed and developing worlds, the connected and disconnected.

In 1961, John F. Kennedy addressed the University of Washington, and in his speech, he spoke of the "long twilight struggle" against Communism—a phrase he used in his Inaugural Address—in which America needed to find the middle way between the extremes of appeasement and war. He envisioned a world where America needed to negotiate gradually toward peace and freedom, from a position of military strength, in a determination to defend its way of life. A long "twilight struggle" has become *our* struggle once again:

Diplomacy and defense are not substitutes for one another. Either alone would fail. For the first time since the ancient battles between Greek city-states, war entails the threat of total annihilation, of everything we know, of society itself. It is customary, both here and around the world, to regard life in the United States as easy. Our advantages are many. But more than any other people on earth, we bear burdens and accept risks unprecedented in their size and their duration, not for ourselves alone but for all who wish to be free. No other generation of free men in any country has ever faced so many and such difficult challenges.

Every word of that speech remains true now, but in a different light. The developed world's crisis, our *new* twilight struggle, requires an urgent, adaptive response from business leadership, negotiating toward productive relationships with other cultures, *from a position of economic strength*—with, at bottom, a new way of thinking about the relationship between developed and underdeveloped cultures, and the way the two relate through trade, commerce, and employment.

As international business leaders, we have the skill set, the experience and capabilities to grow, develop, and add value to our communities, nations, and the global village. We can drive profits and increase standards of living. But we have to change the way we relate to the people around the world who work for us, buy from us, and supply us with their skills and resources. There are new rules to learn, new skills to acquire, all growing out of a new moral compass. Our creative energies need to be focused, with all the passion we can spare, on finding new ways to connect our own way of doing things with the deepest needs of the rest of the world. Our values must be internalized and translated into productive action, from Indonesia to Ecuador. We must connect our own futures with the future of those outside our companies. In a global economy, connecting the disconnected is the most crucial of all the new imperatives facing business in the new century. Freedom and free enterprise are not gifts; they have to be earned and defended by each generation.

To serve as an ambassador to the developing, underprivileged world has become essential in preserving long-term stability in the global economy. It's a role at the heart of free enterprise now: to convince that world that the values and principles of free enterprise are worth following and emulating. Whatever furthers that cause helps build a stronger soil for economic growth both here and around the world—and the global economy has made that geographic distinction nearly meaningless. We *are* the world now.

It behooves the private sector to become diplomats around the world, as individuals, as brands, and as a coalition looking out for the interests of freedom itself. An organization called Business for Diplomatic Action (BDA), created and headed by Keith Reinhard, chairman of DDB Worldwide, has dedicated itself to spearheading a variety of programs to sensitize Americans and their organizations about the rapid decline in the world's opinion of America. It is a worthy experiment that deserves to succeed. Its principles need to be embraced by developed world companies in every nation. In August 2004, Keith addressed the House Subcommittee on National Security, which was seeking recommendations on public diplomacy. He told the committee that the world's opinion of America has plummeted over the past few years as a result of four root causes: U.S. foreign policy, the effects of globalization, the pervasiveness of American popular culture, and the perceived arrogance and ignorance of American individuals.

He quoted British author Margaret Drabble as representative of the kind of nauseated response America evokes now throughout the rest of the world: "My anti-Americanism has . . . possessed me like a disease. I can't keep it down any longer. I detest Disneyfication. I detest Coca-Cola. I detest burgers. I detest sentimental and violent Hollywood movies that tell lies about history."

BDA maintains that private organizations and citizens can do much to change all this. It has produced or proposed roundtables for corporate leaders, an Internet-based virtual library of best practices from U.S. companies that have learned how to become good global citizens, books and pamphlets on how to fit in with foreign cultures and on corporate engagement with foreign countries, and an outreach program to gather information, observations, and insight and build a database of learning about various cultures from actual employees working overseas.

The urgency of connecting with the disconnected can't be overstressed. How we communicate our purposes and behave in other cultures is crucial to whether or not we can defend our ideals. It's a responsibility both private and public, and ultimately crucial both for the future of free enterprise and for the security of the free world.

5

ALIGNMENT

The Magic Word

In the early years of my Y&R career, Ed Ney took over the leadership there. He was a visionary, an enlightened leader by this book's definition and, fortunately for me, my mentor and lifelong supporter. Ed led the company successfully for some sixteen years, becoming the most distinguished and influential person in the industry throughout his career. In the early 1970s, Ed saw how ad agencies needed to offer comprehensive strategic marketing campaigns, not just great advertising. The reason was simple. Ad agencies were increasingly being judged in terms of results. Brilliant execution was meaningless if it was embedded in a flawed strategy—so, under Ed's leadership, we began the journey toward thinking and behaving as strategic business consultants, not just creators of effective advertising. We began to see ourselves as guardians watching over every vehicle through which a client communicated with the world. This new strategic vision required us to entirely reorganize our corporation—it required *alignment*, the coordination of an entire organization's mission toward only one goal: the satisfaction of the client or customer.

Accordingly, Y&R set out to acquire the world's best direct marketing company (Wunderman, Ricotta & Klein), a leading sales promotion firm (Cato Johnson), the most prestigious public relations agency (Burson Marsteller), one of the best medical communications agencies (Sudler & Hennessey), and later, the premier corporate brand identity agency (Landor), as well as other related businesses. I didn't participate in any of the acquisitions during the 1970s. But it was a cutting-edge expansion model, different from what the rest of the industry was doing.

Ed and his brilliant successor, Alex Kroll, another of my coaches and mentors, believed—correctly—that Y&R needed to expand beyond advertising through various media and become a full-service, end-to-end provider of communications strategy: we had to sell *solutions*, not just pieces and parts of a campaign. To take advantage of shifts in the way people would communicate in the future, the advertising business needed to anticipate its own slow decline as the primary way to promote sales of various products. Agencies needed to blend all the various instruments into a smoothly orchestrated service: advertising, public relations, direct marketing, database marketing, sales promotion, merchandising, and all other forms of marketing communications. It was tough. It took more than a couple of decades to make genuine progress, because each silo of expertise competed with the others for a larger share of the client's business.

In the early nineties, when I was about to become CEO myself after nearly thirty years at Y&R, as much as I believed in the solutions model embedded in this full-service concept, I was still instinctively uneasy about how it led to a steady increase in the agency's size. I feared growth would make it harder for us to react quickly to shifting demands. Even worse, I could see it threatening our culture. The internal strife our growth generated was making the agency an uncomfortable place to work. I sensed the only way to stay focused on the client was to create smoothly functioning teams within Y&R—build cross-functional teams dedicated exclusively to a given client, offering fully integrated solutions, with participants from every discipline working toward common goals.

This idea crystallized in my mind when we tried to decide how to handle our account with Lincoln Mercury. I had just become CEO, and Lincoln Mercury was our largest account. The automaker was going to introduce the Mercury Villager in 1993, a

van that would function much like an SUV. But it would be difficult to sell this vehicle against its well-entrenched competition. We
had a tremendous stake in this. If the Villager succeeded, Ford
Motor Co. would continue to design for Mercury, and Mercury
would continue to call on us for help. So we had to make the
launch work.

After our first briefing with Lincoln Mercury, we knew that if
we were going to succeed against Chrysler, then the leader and cre-
ator of the SUV category, we'd have to recruit a deep bench of
major talent, the best, brightest, broadest minds at Y&R. Ford was
a latecomer. We had to try a new approach, so we asked our client
if we could bring other experts to the next meeting. They didn't
care who we brought, as long as those people brought results.

Next time, under the leadership of Satish Korde, one of Y&R's
best minds and one of the most effective managers ever, at the table
we had reps from every major company I just mentioned under the
Y&R umbrella. Thus was born Team Mercury. It was also the birth
of the full-service integrated solution. As a coordinated team, we
studied the behavior of different market segments and worked backward from behavior to attitudes. From attitudes, we designed different campaigns for different groups:

The Soccer Mom: chauffeuring the team

The Young: lugging bikes, skis, kayaks, and tents

The Older Fans: tailgating at the Sunday game

The Builders: carrying loads in a utility truck

The prevailing wisdom was that the big money was with the
Young. But that segment was the most competitive, so we decided
to approach them as only one of several groups. We balanced our
efforts by fanning out into the other groups, using every arrow in
our quiver—magazines for the Young, television for Soccer Moms,
direct mail and public relations for the others. We picked the most
cost-efficient media for each market segment.

It worked. The Villager was a hit. We didn't just promise results: we got them. The notion of *team client* began to emerge as a construct for the whole agency—a matrix for all our major clients. This wouldn't have happened if we hadn't had a clear measure of our effect on Mercury's business. By using the Brand Asset Valuator, we proved our worth to the client by showing exactly how much progress we'd made on building the brand. In other words, our fundamental competencies—our ability to track and measure our results in the most precise way—enabled us to succeed in our strategic vision for the client. Take another step back, for a broader perspective, *all* the principles I've talked about already were the building blocks for alignment—creativity, the enlightened leadership of Ed Ney, our competency in using the Brand Asset Valuator—all made it possible to achieve an integrated solution. To achieve alignment.

As we moved toward alignment in this way, we realized the only way to unify each team client was to change the structure of our entire organization so that this kind of teamwork could emerge. That meant changing almost everything about the way we operated, including our own internal compensation policies. Instead of the different silos of expertise getting paid exclusively for their contribution, we had, as well, to pay everyone based on the impact the *entire* team had on the client's market share or bottom line. Without that crucial change, the old divisive competition between silos would simply replicate itself in miniature within the team. Every faction would try to maximize its own impact—essentially defeating the purpose of the matrix. The focus would have been inward rather than on the client's results.

That willingness to change the internal wiring of rewards created the most powerful way to deliver the integrated solution. Our success through the nineties had everything to do with this approach. We were now paying people to submerge their egos and identify completely with the client's objectives. Clients began to trust us as a company. They didn't know or care who in particular was in the room. Around the major clients or brands, we created a virtual company, a team, of integrated disciplines. The solution and the results it got were all that mattered—not determining who should get the credit. As a result, the integrated solution differentiated Y&R from all other agencies and drove the most successful campaign to bring in new business in the agency's history.

Then we took things a step further to link client results with agency compensation—and this is where it really got tough. We argued, successfully, that a client should pay *us* based on the quality of our results and our impact on the brand. At Y&R, our "profit-sharing plan," or annual incentive, was founded on annual objectives agreed upon by employees and their immediate supervisors. The same model, essentially, can be applied to the way a client compensates the agency itself. Most agencies still base agency compensation on a percentage of a client's total spending on ad space and media time. The more media the agency purchases for a client, the more money it makes. It's illogical, unreasonable, and unfair to clients. Keith Reinhard of DDB Worldwide and I—without being aware of each other's activities—independently developed the concept of *gain sharing*, a value-driven compensation system in which the agency shares in the upside potential of a client's success. This concept had always been rejected in the past because it's difficult to isolate the effect of advertising on a brand. But as marketing grew in importance—and, again, with the BAV to demonstrate our results—we had an opportunity, through gain sharing, to truly align the interests of clients and agency for the first time.

In the mid-1990s, Keith and I began to push some of our respective clients toward the gain-sharing compensation system. Here's how it worked at Y&R. The client agrees on a base fee, which is a negotiated annual dollar amount including a certain base profit for Y&R. From there, the agency may be compensated more, if certain negotiated criteria are met, such as increases in sales, market share, profit, and even the client's stock price. Usually a combination of all these factors is used, along with some qualitative measures, such as the perceived quality of the work. The Brand Asset Valuator can be applied to the client's business to measure, in a precise way, the effect of our work: how it has helped differentiate the brand in a relevant way, raised its esteem, and increased knowledge of what the company can do for customers.

This has been a hard sell, at times. Internally, to a certain extent, you can decree rapid change. But clients have the annoying habit of wanting to be persuaded. That takes time. By the time I left the agency, less than a quarter of Y&R clients used the gain-sharing system, but slowly more and more of them were seeing how the old commission system had a cancerous potential. Every time the agency pushed for a new initiative in marketing or advertising, its intent would be questioned: "Here comes the agency again, pushing for more spending and a bigger commission." The result was a highly adversarial and contentious relationship. The gain-sharing solution produced a healthier bond between client and agency: it's win-win, or nobody gains. That's alignment in a nutshell.

Some corporate changes can begin from the bottom up. The gain-sharing compensation system is *not* an example. You have to be the CEO to push something like this through. Changing an entire industry is a difficult process. Nonetheless, gain sharing was steadily winning converts. Once a skeptical division president asked me how I could create fair criteria for judging the effect of an agency's work on a client's results. I asked him, "How does your board decide the size of your annual bonus?" He said, "That's simple. It's a function of revenue growth, profitability, and stock price."

"There you go," I said.

The Integrated Solution

Alignment is the critical concept for the twenty-first-century enterprise. It integrates all the other principles of this book, because an aligned company integrates everything it does around its mission. An enterprise that draws freely upon all internal knowledge and resources to deliver a superior product or service is aligned. Its competencies, its creative firepower, and its vision, values, ethics, and integrity are harmonized and coordinated. Second, when an organization holds fast to the concept of alignment, it will integrate what it does so that it serves the interests of all its critical stakeholders. An aligned company does only what is in the interests of these groups, from employees to customers, from shareholders to financial analysts, as well as the communities and governments it serves. As a result, an aligned company not only produces high-quality products or services, it becomes responsible to the world around it.

Alignment in both senses must be a management imperative. It cannot be left to chance. It is not the serendipitous by-product of everyone's striving hard to do a good job. To achieve it often requires significant change throughout an organization, including changes in some form of matrix management, along with carefully designed reward programs to motivate proper behavior. With alignment, all internal knowledge and resources line up to do only one thing: deliver a superior product or service in an environment of meaningful work.

It may be possible to describe the state of alignment, but it's a bit harder to pin down how you get to it. You can't dissect its parts and get a clear vision of how it works. You have to stretch a bit for comparisons: aligned organizations are like great athletes or artists perfectly synchronized with their era and their audience. There's something holistic about alignment. In an aligned company, an improvement in any area seems to reverberate throughout the rest of the company. Someone once said that good farmers are really in the business of creating beautiful landscapes: those with the greenest fields and the neatest hedgerows also produce the most milk. There may be a causal relationship between a green field and good milk, but that isn't the point: in an aligned organization, every detail of an enterprise reflects the collective passion that makes it superior. Everything relates to and depends on everything else in other parts of that business.

A company organized with stand-alone business units, hermetically sealed silos dedicated to various product lines, will rarely achieve alignment. The company can align itself more easily when it is integrated around *market segments*, if not individual customers or clients. This new, sometimes fluid, matrix must be structured so that teams can assemble to deliver and measure results in the market. Share price, quarterly profit, revenue, productivity, sales goals, cost measures—all of these are now by-products of finding creative new ways to build on the momentum a company achieves by connecting with its market. Internal benchmarks of achievement, interdepartmental rivalries—all of this pales in comparison with the collective delight in working together for customer satisfaction. The compensation structure must reward nothing but outer-directed results. A campaign or initiative that spikes profit or share price for a few quarters but has little or no impact on long-term value delivered to those who buy the product or service will fail to create lasting results.

Alignment is inherently ethical. When an organization achieves it, the new equation of success—*values equal value*—begins to work. In such an organization, ethics equate to earnings. It's an organized way to do good. In the excess supply economy all transactions increasingly depend on trust, which itself depends on honesty and reliable quality. The desired outcome for all business now is customer loyalty. The customer's long-term welfare comes first. To achieve this loyalty, the aligned business looks up to employees and clients and customers, not down at them. This is a shift in values away from self-glorification or rapid gain or tough-guy leadership toward what you could characterize as a kind of profitable altruism.

IBM: High-Performance Culture

Few stories illustrate the challenges and rewards of alignment quite as well as IBM. Nearly a decade ago, Lou Gerstner inherited the company, with its many diverse strengths, and proceeded to align it around a focus on solutions for individual customers. When Gerstner took over IBM on April Fools Day in 1993, though it had a stellar brand and was known for excellence, customer service, and respect for the individual, IBM was mired in bureaucracy and on the verge of disintegrating. He recognized that the PC was going to become a commodity. Gerstner saw alignment as the key to a turnaround—in a unique way. It was a model for a reorganization of his own company, but it was also a concept that would transform the nature of what his company would sell. IBM was selling individual products when he took over but, by the time Gerstner transformed it, it was selling alignment itself in the form of networked solutions. He saw that the mainframe computer could be the centerpiece of a computer network used to align a customer's business.

The common view at the time was that the world of information technology was rocketing toward a new model: "distributed computing" where personal computers, or personal devices—the "clients"—would get more and more powerful, and the best software would be designed to run these personal devices networked to larger "servers." All the computing power would trickle down to the PCs, or PDAs, or someone's wristwatch, as Gerstner put it. The mainframe market—which had always been IBM's cash cow, bringing in 90 percent of revenue—was supposedly dying.

Gerstner believed these prevailing assumptions were too simplistic. He believed networks were the future of computing, not the PC nor the software needed to run it. He'd learned, at American Express and Nabisco, how to differentiate a brand, and he believed he could do it again at IBM. For the market he wanted to reach—organizations like his own—as networks took hold and bandwidth got bigger, he believed much of the value would migrate *upward* away from the client devices into the network and the servers themselves. As a result, he decided to bet on the mainframe and unify the company around its strength—as the most powerful "server" possible in a networked world. Rather than break up IBM into smaller, tougher units, he saw a completely new opportunity for his company to align *itself,* pulling together all of IBM's diverse strengths to become a full-service provider of solutions. It could then move in and help customers network and integrate all the diverse elements of their computing world.

At the time, few people other than Gerstner recognized this. The press mocked him as he announced the mainframe would remain a cornerstone of revenue. Then their jaws dropped as he lowered the price of his mainframe, which meant an immediate and dramatic loss in revenue. (Obviously, his unspoken assumption was that even the IBM mainframe had become a commodity, but he never uttered this blasphemy—even as he acted on the truth of it.)

In software, he moved the focus to "middleware," which then was an obscure stratum of the market. Middleware is code that coordinates and integrates—again, *integration*—all the different processes going on in the network, all the different applications, users, and systems. He announced that everything in the company would be aligned by building customized, integrated solutions around the mainframe, using IBM's own middleware to link together all parts of a network. IBM would use competitors' products in these solutions, if necessary—slipping them, as needed, into various gaps in the proposed solution. Devalue the mainframe? Deemphasize the PC? Quit pushing IBM's own stellar operating system? Buy and resell a competitor's products? It seemed to some people Gerstner was out of his mind. Or living in another world. He was. It happened to be the *real* world. He simply had the vision to recognize where he was.

IBM's mainframe sales began to grow and have continued to grow. And its Software Group, on the strength of middleware, has become the leading software company in networked computing. IBM became an IT consultant, selling its wisdom and expertise in building customized solutions. In *Who Says Elephants Can't Dance*, Gerstner writes: "You sell a capability. You sell knowledge. You create it at the same time you deliver it. The business model is different. The economics are entirely different" (p. 133).

IBM is one of the great comebacks in corporate history. Along the way, IBM also developed a brilliant communication campaign created by my esteemed competitors at Ogilvy and Mather to trumpet the new IBM and align it with customers' needs. It was a most convincing and effective effort. The comeback was an epic challenge, but the strategy worked. It took years to reorganize the company. "It involved millions of dollars of investments, thousands of hours of work, and, eventually, changed the way tens of thousands of IBMers worked" (p. 232). What this kind of effort generates is what Gerstner calls a "high-performance culture," or what anthropologist Joseph Campbell called the "Great Good Place." When every employee has a passion for the business, just walking into that culture is like being immersed in a brighter, more aware, more creative world. You know it as soon as you come into contact with anyone who works in that kind of company.

Gerstner formed a clear vision of a new market and a new way of doing business, and he abandoned all effort that didn't serve this market. He elevated successful execution to the highest status because it was where IBM's solutions either succeeded or failed— and where, as a result, the company succeeded or failed. The key was to align competencies to customers' needs through operational excellence. And the final alignment was measuring results for individual customers and not just IBM. Ultimately, the source of success for Gerstner and IBM rested on this magical win-win alignment.

A Tale of Two Airlines

This is the story of two airlines, one new, one old. One aligned and successful, one misaligned and struggling to stay alive.

JetBlue *began* as an aligned company, with no cultural legacy to transform. It has focused entirely on what its customers want. By offering the lowest fares available and creating a culture that ingratiates itself with every individual flier, JetBlue has managed to soar in an industry struggling to get its jets off the ground. It took to the air in February 2000 and began making a profit eight months later. Granted, the airline has a pool of venture capital from its IPO and major investors, including George Soros, to help it weather any downturn. And it has only the infrastructure it needs, with a fleet of new jets, a fresh workforce, and a business model that has worked well for Southwest Airlines. It has stayed regional, and has grown carefully.

JetBlue has built an internal culture that generates customer loyalty. It has created a new kind of brand identity in the skies— reliable, cheerful, and inexpensive—in an era when travel has become synonymous with unpleasant surprises and dismal service. JetBlue is completely aligned toward the customer. Ticket agents are chipper. Flight attendants and pilots could be described as almost light-hearted. Each passenger has a private television. It's an airline that makes you *want* to fly in an industry that has made air travel something to dread. JetBlue is a terrific success story. But the airline is young. It hasn't been tested by time, aging aircraft, and the risks of growing too fast, too big, when it might begin to replicate problems now faced by the current majors. But so far, so good.

United Airlines is the second airline story. Poor management and deregulation have weakened many airlines to the point where they are the first victims of stagnation, many now struggling in the throes of bankruptcy. United Airlines is a good example. What's ironic is how much UAL *ought* to have been aligned. It had an enlightened leader, and management and workers were running the company together. Everyone was on the same team. In 1994, an employee stock ownership plan gave workers a 55 percent stake in the parent UAL Corporation and the control that came with it. The unions had enough seats on the board to maintain the right to veto major business decisions, and they had final say over the selection of the company's chief executive.

Employee ownership was a great idea, but it was badly executed. CEO Gerry Greenwald was extraordinary: tough-minded, fair, smart—a world-class leader. He originated the plan to give employees stock ownership. He wanted them to have a stake in the company's success. It was a plan designed to promote teamwork, yet—as it turned out—the incentive to collaborate evaporated and created tensions and misalignment.

The plan worked fine while the UAL stock was going up. When the stock and the stock market both started to go south, the entire calculus of the relationship went sour. Employees gave substantial concessions to gain share ownership. But when share prices declined, their sacrifices turned out to be worthless and even worse. Employees couldn't do anything to change their situation, so they became bitter. The airline was dropping below industry standards by most measures. Labor leaders on the board of directors, biased toward the interests of the employees they represented, attempted to protect wages and job security. When Greenwald was preparing to retire in 1998, the person in line to take over for him was John Edwardson, an outstanding executive and exemplary human being, but the unions rejected him, because he was a tough manager who understood the crucial need to cut labor costs. Instead, Jim Goodwin became CEO in 1998, and his mandate was clear: to fix the company without touching the labor cost structure. As a result, UAL led itself into disaster—and eventually bankruptcy.

In the misaligned battle between management, shareholders, and employees, the interests of UAL's customers—the flying public—were left out of the picture. An aligned business cannot be focused only on money. While it must measure its success by profits and share price, that's not the force that creates value. What the philosopher John Stuart Mill discovered, more than a century ago, about happiness—it isn't an end to be pursued but rather the almost accidental *effect* of pursuing a worthy outcome—applies perfectly here. Genuinely happy people don't really chase happiness. They're too busy doing what they love doing. The really profitable companies are on fire with a certain kind of zeal—and it isn't simply about profit. That's what Bill George did at Medtronic, as outlined in Chapter Three. The first order of business is to add value, for the customer's benefit—and, in this new economic world, the only way to do that is to translate the right competence and character into organizational *practice*. The profits can follow if you first delight the customer and then skillfully practice the art and science of extracting the earnings from healthy revenues. That is the essence of alignment.

Alignment requires a company to take the customer's needs to heart. People actually have to *care*. They can't just read from a script that forces them through the motions. Almost every book that offers advice on how to do business focuses on skills and practices—mechanistic, repeatable techniques. The reality of what happens in a successful business, the living soul of a beautifully coordinated business, gets boiled down to a tick sheet of to-dos. *Do this and this and that—and you'll succeed!* It's all mechanical. The problem is that success is no longer simply about tactics, and therefore it's no longer teachable in the abstract, in the sense that a list of best practices can be taught.

Greatness doesn't come from just mastering fragmented areas of competence. While competence *is* essential, and while there is no substitute for flawless execution, it's no longer sufficient. Success now has as much to do with who you are, the unique and moral character your people bring to their work, and the way it governs the way you care for customers—because that trustworthy character is what customers look for now in a company. The source of success comes from passion and discipline and being directed outward toward *someone other than yourself*: age-old earmarks of greatness, in a way that eventually generates profit.

I return to these personal values in the next chapter. But alignment in its broader sense encompasses all these critical elements of business in the new excess supply economy.

To Clothe the World

Levi Strauss and Co. (LS&Co.) is an intriguing story of the company in transit from the old excess demand world to the new excess supply economy. In the old world, LS&Co. was king of the denim business. It almost monopolized the industry. Things became so easy thanks to the brilliance of the original founders and the extraordinary demand, which far exceeded supply. But too much of a good thing created a powerful, hungry, aggressive group of competitors. And the loose competencies installed during the easy times were inadequate in the new economic world order. The firm's very survival was at stake.

LS&Co. has moved a long way toward alignment in a few short years—with a sense of urgency other companies would do well to heed. Today, it's an organization with an extremely simple and outrageously daring mission—to clothe the world. It's in the process of turning itself around and appears to have strong prospects for growth, built on one of the most familiar and trusted brands: Levi's jeans. It sells in over a hundred countries, and it still has one of the most trusted brands in apparel. Levi Strauss offers an impressive illustration of how values can and must be translated into organizational structure and process.

Only three years ago, even *Fortune* magazine was lamenting LS&Co. as a management failure. "In April of '99, *Fortune* called us a *failed Utopian management experiment,* and said our focus on values contributed to our problem. That's baloney. We took our eye off the marketplace," says Phil Marineau, CEO. "LS&Co. is a phe-nomenally responsible employer and company. And that's exactly what makes our brand strong."

It may have been a strong brand, but the magazine was right about one thing: it wasn't making nearly enough money. Levi's jeans used to be the only brand anyone wanted to buy. In 1996, sales peaked at $7.1 billion and then began to plummet. It was a classic story of a company gripped by the momentum of false confi-dence built on the premium quality of its brand. Over the past decade, though LS&Co. watched as one new competitor after another nibbled away at its market share, it continued to believe it could do no wrong. It ignored changing tastes and the need to operate with much greater humility than in the past. By the mid-nineties, it was desperate for alignment, but didn't begin to move toward it until 1999, when Bob Haas, the company's part-owner and chairman, brought in CEO Phil Marineau.

Marineau began a program to wake up his organization to the excess supply economy and push everyone to change the way they operated.

> We're driven by our own past failure to really deal with two funda-mental issues. The first is that there are hundreds more brands than used to exist. Two hundred more brands than ten years ago. You have to distinguish with product innovation or you allow your brand to become commoditized. The apparel business over twenty years has had twenty years of deflation, chasing low-cost labor outside the U.S., to engage all this new competition with lower prices. We have now closed all of our U.S. plants, as humanely as possible, I hope. It will enable us to offer our retailers a much greater margin.
>
> We've also begun selling outside our usual channels. In the past, we sold through department stories—Penney's, May, Federated, and Sears. The emergence of mass merchants, like Wal-Mart, and specialty retailing, like PacSun or Urban Outfitters, has changed everything.

The competition this creates is what I call the Jaws of Death. We needed to react to these changes, and we didn't have a clear focus. The new order created chaos in the organization. In the past, demand always exceeded supply, so we could replenish the supply on our own terms. We had a lousy plan for dealing with supply chain management.

Marineau taught the company to innovate and lead from the core business, not straying from pants until sales were solid and growing again. It hasn't looked outside the core business for solutions to its problems.

Second, LS&Co. has revitalized retail relationships. "We fixed the product, with a dependable supply. We're much easier to do business with now. We plan with customers individually to track buying patterns and plan to supply them exactly what they'll need, so they'll never run out."

Third, sell where people shop. "We've expanded our distribution in specialty stores, in malls, in PacSun, Urban Outfitters. And, on the other end, we have started to sell successfully Levi Strauss Signature Jeans in Wal-Mart and Target."

Fourth, operate with excellence. LS&Co. has developed a complex and sophisticated ability to project demand with the goal that no customer will go to any point of purchase looking for a specific line, in a certain color and size, and fail to find it. It's an enormous challenge. "We've gone from being absolutely miserable to being best in class. We have close information sharing with the retailers, and we use IT systems that enable us to track and analyze and therefore predict buying patterns. We tailor what we provide to the exact specifications of each individual customer: each retailer."

Finally, the company has a clear strategic intent. It's learning to work *The LS&Co. Way.* "We stand for empathy, originality, integrity and courage. The character of the company and our values have sustained us in the tailspin. *People love our clothes and trust our company. We will clothe the world.* Those lines from the *LS&Co.*

Way energize the company and becomes the platform on which you build your goals."

It hasn't been easy. Marineau, at times, was a lonely man. When he realized the company had to sell through mass merchandisers such as Wal-Mart, only a few people approved. Rather than force acquiescence and agreement, he managed opinion throughout the organization by offering the data to everyone, enabling them to recognize the truth.

"You have to execute with patience *and* impatience. I knew we had to go to Wal-Mart. But it was like running into battle with nobody following. You had to let them reach the conclusions themselves. This requires patience. So, how do you do this, but still be *impatient?*" That's the CEO challenge for Phil Marineau, Ken Rollins at Dell, and every successful CEO.

The LS&Co. tale is indeed a work in progress. What Phil Marineau describes is the need to instill in his company every principle outlined in this book: have a strong and clear strategic intent, build basic competencies, be outwardly focused—respecting competition and figuring out how to innovate and differentiate the brand. Vitally important, alignment became Phil Marineau's mantra. Align with consumers' ever-changing needs for style and functionality. Aligning with existing retail interests—get them higher margins and make it easier for them to work with LS&Co. Align with the emerging retailers where its customers shop: Wal-Mart, Target, and Kmart. Aligning the internal organization to deliver best practices to every corner of the enterprise. And these alignment efforts were executed while maintaining the highest level of integrity in the way it performed its business everywhere in the world. And it did so making very tough calls while being fair. Tough yes, mean-spirited no.

Phil Marineau certainly feels the CEO is responsible for driving alignment throughout the organization. LS&Co. has made serious progress against its turnaround mission. It may not be time to declare final victory, but then, in the new economic world order, victory only comes when you best your competitors with better, differentiated products and have the ability to make good profits from those satisfied customers—day in and day out, year after year.

But for now, no one is talking about failed Utopian management experiments any more.

A Company That Almost Runs Itself

At IBM and Levi Strauss and Co.—as well as Dell, Amazon, eBay, and many other great companies that have emerged in the past decade—organizations found ways of aligning themselves around the needs of individual customers partly by translating strength of character into organizational practice. Once alignment begins to emerge, a new spirit infuses an organization. The outward focus it achieves releases enormous creativity and energy through the actions of every worker. Few companies have exemplified how alignment generalizes strong character—distributing it to nearly everyone in the company—quite as effectively as Verizon did during the 9/11 attack on the World Trade Center. The Verizon story shows how all the principles of this book can contribute, in an extraordinary way, to creative solutions—at an almost heroic level. It illustrates competence, respect, integrity, caring, and the enlightened leadership that created this culture in the first place and then kept it alive when it was most needed.

Until September 11, 2001, the giant telecommunications firm had talked a good game about serving communities. On that day and in the weeks afterward, it lived up to its word. Ivan Seidenberg, speaking for himself and for Chuck Lee, his co-CEO at Verizon at that time, puts it this way:

> On September 11, the vision and the values were both put to the test. Initially, the company was obsessed with getting its 2,200 workers in the Trade Center to safety. Once employees were evacuated, the firm

made sure its switching facility was operational, so that emergency services to the area wouldn't be interrupted. The systems operated until later in the day when flooding became a problem. But the larger crisis was how to restore cellular services to 14,000 businesses and 20,000 residential customers: the attack had destroyed ten cellular towers and 300,000 voice lines, along with 3.6 million data circuits. With an emergency command center, we kept communications working for 911, police, fire, and rescue operations. But the larger challenge was to keep our regular customers as connected as they'd been before the attack.

This is where the company's inherent organizational creativity became crucial. Through thousands of improvised decisions in the midst of the crisis, at all levels from the bottom up, Verizon made its vision a reality. The value of service, the ideal of serving all people who depended on the company for reliable communication, giving everyone in the corporation a deep and meaningful sense of purpose—this is what enabled these largely unsupervised people to connect and communicate, allowing the company to come alive for customers in unexpected ways. As Seidenberg puts it: "No emergency command center could have directed all the actions of all these people in such chaos. Those on-the-spot decisions, which were inherently creative, had to be made on instinct, and that's where an organization's values really get tested."

The priorities narrowed down to three simple principles: Take care of employees. Take care of customers. Take care of the community.

These principles governed everything Verizon did during the crisis, because everyone in the company had internalized them. Principles and values became the foundation and essence of Verizon's competence in this crisis. They created a spirit of self-discipline at all levels and enabled everyone to leverage their deepest creativity. Throughout the nightmare of the weeks following the attack, as Verizon restored full service at all levels, Seidenberg and

Lee went to the site repeatedly to meet with workers and encourage them, listen to their stories, and sympathize. They hugged people. They shook hands.

"People cried on my shoulder as they told me of seeing bodies plummet from buildings, and somehow these same people still went back to work. They talked about their fear of the future," he says.

But these were brief work breaks in the midst of a marathon effort to create new ways to reconnect customers and businesses that depended on telecommunications to recover, essentially, a way of life that depended on the capital markets, which had been brought to a halt by the attack. As Ivan puts it, "Nothing epitomized our commitment like our effort to reopen the New York Stock Exchange on September 17, only six days after the attack."

That effort involved restoring 2 million data circuits and 1.5 million phone lines in less than a week, a job that would ordinarily have taken months. To achieve this involved nothing less than enormous courage from workers: ten employees wearing moon suits and respirators walked up two dozen flights of stairs in one facility to retrieve servers containing the software that transmitted quotes to the Exchange floor. Computer technicians reprogrammed a system that had been set up a decade earlier. Verizon Wireless gave out five thousand cell phones to rescue workers and brought in seven "cells-on-wheels" to restore critical wireless services.

"And for six days, around the clock, hundreds of telephone technicians, working alongside rescue workers, lay cable, pulled phone lines through windows seven floors up, hand-cleaned equipment covered with soot and ash," Seidenberg says. "On the spot, all these workers improvised ways to rebuild the communication infrastructure for lower Manhattan."

Once trading resumed on the NYSE, the company still needed to restore service to thirty-four thousand affected businesses and residences, which meant monitoring the status of customers on an hourly basis. "We hit the streets. We met personally with public housing tenants and set up special offices for them and other residences. We made free cell phones available with six hours of free calling. We walked into small businesses, distributing informative flyers. We set up toll-free numbers in Spanish and Chinese. We took out public service ads in papers. And we posted information about critical services, like call forwarding and voice mail, on our Web site."

The company brought the same kind of commitment to the community at large by offering thousands of employees to staff call centers to help raise more than $150 million for victims and their families. Everything Verizon did was a consequence of the company's state of alignment: nothing was too extreme, too risky, or too generous if it served the needs of customers in crisis. Creative solutions sprang up at all levels, throughout the company. This is alignment at its best.

As Seidenberg acknowledges candidly, "We, the leadership of the company, didn't dictate any of the tens of thousands of decisions that had to be made in those critical forty-eight hours to achieve all these things. These choices arose spontaneously in the field, in real time, as workers created new ways to serve customers and citizens and one another. The culture of this company made that kind of empowerment possible."

Verizon risked short-term losses to stay true to its core values and built a relationship of trust that will drive profits for years to come. It has been ascending ever since.

What these examples show is that alignment begins internally: to align mission and vision with a customer's desires, an entire company must, essentially, play a concert for an audience of one. All aspects of the business must act as part of the orchestra. There are no soloists in the aligned company, and the conductor is only as good as the ability of every musician to keep time with all the others. Alignment can be achieved in a few years, but it isn't a steady state. It requires continuous readjustments, and it evolves into different forms over time. As the environment changes, as competition shifts, as business strategies grow more subtle, alignment must adapt to these changes. It must always be part of the success model.

Companies often regress from huge success to average performance (or worse), and more often than not this change means alignment has begun to slip. If the concept is not institutionalized, when management changes or when business changes, it can be lost, ignored, or forgotten. Working as a team, emphasizing "we" over "me," is never instinctive. The culture quickly reverts and soon the organization is struggling to sell commodities. Alignment begins and endures only with enlightened leadership. All the leaders I've mentioned—Lou Gerstner, Ed Ney, Phil Marineau, Ivan Seidenberg and Chuck Lee, and many more I have had the good fortune to work with over the years—are ethical, honest leaders who govern with respect and integrity. They have recognized that excellence follows from a new way of leading organizations. Alignment can't achieve its fullest expression without that kind of leadership.

6

VALUES

Dare to Be Good

At Young & Rubicam, I was a walking American Dream. I started with the company right out of school, and I rose steadily into more and more rewarding positions. In my early thirties, it seemed, anything was possible. Yet for all my happiness and success, all was not well with me. As I began to move up in the organization, I also began to feel my confidence eroding, without understanding why. Fear and foreboding welled up within me, suddenly and unexpectedly, in ways I'd never experienced even in my childhood. Walking down Madison Avenue one day, I was filled with dread—something that had been happening more and more often over the previous weeks. I kept walking. I stopped so abruptly a woman bumped into me from behind. I looked around. Out of the torrent of New Yorkers, on the sidewalks, I heard a voice: "Hey. Look!"

I gazed straight up at a man on a window ledge of an office building directly above me, swaying there in the breeze. I looked away immediately and started running. I wanted to get as far from that man as quickly as I could. I turned a corner and kept running, expecting to hear the screams of horror from the crowd behind me. But I didn't. I went home that night and I knew that, unlike that man on the window ledge, I was falling already and had no idea how to reach out and grasp anything to break the fall.

I'm almost hesitant to admit this was not an entirely abnormal day for me, back then. My dread and anxiety had been growing stronger and stronger over the preceding months. Career failure, loss of my job, poverty were the worst fates I could imagine, and I was sure my hard work would see me through all those dangers. Nonetheless, I was full of fear. My personality was, to put it mildly, an emotional and psychological jumble of conflicting beliefs and pragmatic assumptions, without a spiritual center.

It began with insomnia. I would wake up and not be able to fall back asleep. Then I started suffering from frequent headaches. I became claustrophobic in elevators and even in bathroom stalls. My attacks became more and more frequent. I became deathly afraid of flying after my friend Joe Curren was killed in a plane crash en route to Cincinnati, where I'd been flying two or three times a week. I became hypersensitive to the feelings of people around me. That kind of awareness can be a good thing to have—but in my case, I became so preoccupied with the way other people felt that it turned into a painful obsession.

I had no religious practice to hold me up—in other words, I had no source of energy and drive outside my own personality and ego. I hadn't lost my belief in God, but God was not a part of my everyday awareness. I belonged to no church. I was, essentially, losing all sense of the *meaning* in my life. I went to doctors, who prescribed medicines that did nothing for me. I didn't consider psychotherapy because I didn't think of myself, in a strict sense, as mentally ill. I knew, instinctively, I was struggling with a spiritual crisis only I could resolve—a reintegration of my personality around a new center. My wife, Barbara—we'd been married a number of years by then—began to believe I was on the verge of a nervous breakdown.

Clearly the source of my anxiety and malaise was rooted deep in my personality and the experiences of my life; therefore what brought it up to the surface, what triggered my crisis, seems ridiculously insignificant. The catalyst, the final pressure point that pushed me into a completely new outlook on life, was what I saw happening to a man I served at Y&R. I'll call him Art McArdle. He had been overlooked for a promotion he deserved. I loved

the man, and his fate at Y&R dealt a crushing blow to my assumptions about human nature. This moment was a turning point for
me, as I watched my hero become a nobody to the people who
employed him.

In my short time at the company, I'd become Art's protégé. I
could always trust him not to laugh at me if I asked a dumb question, and I was still in that awkward newbie stage where all the
questions I asked probably sounded dumb to most of those around
me. He was, in a sense, a father to me in the organization.

When I learned Art was getting a new manager, it didn't make
sense. What was happening shook my most fundamental beliefs about
work. He got passed over, even though he was the most qualified to
move up. It was a mystery to all of us why he didn't get the job. He
deserved the most senior position in the account. Everyone was convinced it was just business, the political maneuvers that bring this sort
of thing about, and had little to do with Art's abilities or qualifications.
Yet no matter how good Art was, and no matter how hard he worked,
it couldn't save him. The people above Art were connected—and so
was the man who got the job Art deserved—and Art wasn't.

You can get ahead by using people—by managing them in a way
that destroys their spirit, and you can go home at night, sleep
soundly, and believe you are a good executive, hard as nails, a man
or a woman who gets things done. It's the classic way to look at how
people get ahead in business. You shed blood, and you don't look
back. You grow up. You learn the rules of the jungle, and then you
play by them. If you aren't tough enough for it, then get out. It's a
question of survival, that's all—the thinking goes—and survival
involves some unpleasant things. Life is tough, fine, no argument
there. But when justice and truth get sacrificed in little ways on the
altar of office politics, something dark finds its way into the daily

routine. In the crucible of character when you must have faith in your own people and risk your own credibility by standing behind them—when a good man gets overlooked, purposely, because someone has more to gain or less to lose by promoting those less qualified, then something even darker slithers into the bright, clean, cost-efficient cycles of business.

Unconsciously, I knew the injustice done to Art had implications for my own future—and this knowledge undermined, in a subtle but crucial way, everything I believed. It precipitated in me a breakdown disproportionate to its cause. A good man had gotten passed over for promotion, that was all, and yet I was losing my grip on everything that gave my life meaning. Every day I felt I was falling into an abyss, without understanding what it meant—nothing had meaning for me. I had to find a way to break my own fall, and then I had to understand *why* all this was happening to me.

Help came in the most offhand, accidental way imaginable. In the midst of this spiritual crisis, on a Sunday morning in 1967, Barbara looked up from the *New York Times* and tossed a section of the paper to me, folded to an advertisement that caught her attention. I put down my tea.

Lower your pulse rate and blood pressure—learn your way to better health.

It was an advertisement for a program run by a man named Jose Silva, someone who had taken Eastern techniques of meditation and brought them to people in a nonsectarian way, stripped of their religious trappings and honed down to practices—the way yoga is often practiced—that gave people the ability to bring their bodies and minds back into a state of restorative harmony. I didn't know any of this at the time. As sad and embarrassing as it seems now—a commentary on how desperate I'd become—this tiny newspaper ad, with its specious-sounding promises, made me intensely curious. I sensed that this obscure, esoteric program might help me get control of my life.

I signed up for the entire course, four days of instruction, twelve hours each day. Later on, I took a more advanced course. So, over weeks and then months, I learned how to meditate, in a time when it was almost a hip thing to do—back when the Beatles were learn- ing it from the Maharishi. The practice, for many, seemed little more than a fad for long-haired college slackers, but I took to it the way a dieter takes to Air Force calisthenics. The practice of meditation has recently made a comeback—with national news magazines doing cover stories on its growing popularity.

I started meditating, but I also started jogging. After months of practice, I learned to relax quickly and easily, both physically and mentally. I developed the habit of doing relaxation techniques and then meditation for an hour every day—as I deepened my daily running habit—and, as a result, my blood pressure and heart rate got lower, and my emotional problems slowly abated. I was losing my fear of failure, and I found myself having more fun at work and taking the inevitable setbacks less personally. I developed a resilient sense of quiet confidence.

Over the next twenty-five years, meditation helped me survive—and win—in my career, through a form of behavior that wasn't simply about serving myself. It gave me the courage to look closely at myself, my own nature, my past, the way I reacted to threatening events—and reassess all of them. I came to realize that my spiritual crisis, triggered by the injustice of Art McArdle's career misfortunes, was out of proportion to the cause.

But I also saw it wasn't crazy. Behind it lay childhood experi- ences I hadn't fully understood. I'd suppressed these memories for years, in my focus on personal survival. I realized I needed to grap- ple with the origin of these overpowering fears I didn't quite under- stand. To move forward in my life, I had to move backward. I had to draw up the most frightening memories of my childhood, what I'd experienced in Romania after the Communists took over the country and put me and my brother to work in a series of degrading jobs. It was where I'd learned my work ethic, but it was also where my experience wounded me more deeply in ways I was only now beginning to understand. It was there where I first saw normal people do evil things. The arrest and then murder of my grandfather, the imprisonment of my grandmother, forcing two young boys into hard labor without education, blackmailing our parents with the lives of their own children. A frightening lesson about human nature was buried in what happened to me during those years, and I had to grasp it before I could move on.

But the deepest and most enduring lesson in all of this, for me as a business executive, was the link I'd discovered between my own personal state of being and the new ways I could lead an organization embedded within this spiritual change in myself. I began to see that my own personal spiritual condition, my entire set of values and beliefs, my character as a person, was the key to my ability to lead other people. It was my deepest and most lasting lesson in values. It was when I began to learn how I had to be a good, whole human being before I could be a good leader.

It's All About Values

In the past, the sort of moral qualities of a good husband or wife, a good father or mother, weren't gritty enough for the bare-knuckle world of business. It was quietly considered a requirement of success that you put on your game face along with your necktie or makeup and leave some of your scruples at home. That kind of split personality, which made it possible for an individual to be both a nurturing parent and a ruthless negotiator, was prized. If you could *compartmentalize* your life, you were in great demand. It was almost an adaptive necessity.

Not anymore. The sort of leader required by this economy lives one life and shows the same face to everyone—and the pleasant surprise, here, is that the person you are required to be is also the person you will *want* to be. The simple way to put it is that in order to be an effective leader, you have to learn to simply be your most authentic self, in all situations, with all people. The new economic world offers you, essentially, the opportunity to quit acting a role in favor of being true to yourself. You can now be one person, every-where, in all things. The family man and enlightened leader gain strength from the same set of values now.

Business easily takes on the ethos of a sport where winning is everything. And sports, as noted earlier, tap into the most atavistic survival instincts, equating winning with survival—where, down through history, survival has meant defeating something or someone else. In sports, by definition, somebody has to win and somebody has to lose. This isn't true in business. It isn't a zero-sum game. You don't kill or vanquish your competitors. You coexist with them, each of you focusing on what you do best. You get desired results by striving for excellence as much as by blocking your opponent's best shots. In the game of business, you win the customer's satisfaction, not your competitor's defeat. Your competitor may fall, but that isn't the point. Focus on that fight against others in the market, and you lose the relationship with your customers, your profit, and your success. There's a different culture you set up in an organization that is more sustainable. In the long term, it will continue to produce better results and is essential for building the relationships of trust and loy-alty with employees and customers required by the new economy.

We can and must adopt basic human values to guide both per-sonal and business behaviors: honesty, trust, respect for others and ourselves, integrity, and accountability. These are generally self-evident, though very difficult to put into practice every day, every time. Two of them deserve brief elaboration. The need to respect yourself is less obvious as a values imperative. But ask yourself whether you can trust the good in others, whether you can appre-ciate the heroic journey of your fellow human beings, if you haven't experienced that goodness within yourself. To be at peace with others you must understand and respect your own struggles and your own progress on the long, never-ending road toward the good.

Accountability, in addition to being a sense of ownership for one's actions, draws a distinction between intent and outcomes. You have to be accountable for your outcomes and their consequences. That is the full meaning of accountability: in fact, you must be responsible for the final *results* of your actions, regardless of how good your intentions were, in your business and personal life.

We can change ourselves for the better by practicing and applying these disciplines, mustering the rigor and commitment of top athletes. That means adhering to the most basic values in dozens of small and large decisions every day. A moral leader is what you're trying to be, but let's not kid ourselves: it takes practice. When the pressure is on, and you have much to lose, maybe—*maybe*—you'll do the right thing. If you do, it will bear fruit for both your reputation and your company's, the strength of your brand, and your business success.

The Tough Calls

Our efforts to inculcate the right values at Y&R didn't always work. As a result, I faced one of the thorniest ethical decisions I've ever had to tackle. In our traffic department, we hired coordinators out of college. It's a good way of getting to know the business. You work with everyone and attend many of the critical meetings. Most go on to become assistant account executives, and many have launched extremely successful advertising careers.

One day, a few of these bright new recruits started to receive e-mail from friends at other agencies that contained racially demeaning jokes. They passed them along, thinking they were funny. A young African American colleague received one of these e-mail messages and was understandably offended. He took the e-mail to Charlee Taylor Hines, who was then a senior executive in the

Research Department and one of Y&R's most senior black executives. She's now at Pepsi Cola: a brilliant woman with a great reputation for integrity and a good friend.

She immediately understood the ethical dimensions of the problem. "Y&R prides itself on its opposition to bigotry," she said, "and here is a horrible example of bigotry at its worst." She reported the incident on our hotline, and the appropriate machinery within the company quickly began to move. Within a couple of days, Y&R's general counsel, Stephanie Abramson (one of my wisest counselors) came into my office along with Bambi Cummings, a lawyer who works for her, dealing with harassment and other labor issues.

They laid out the facts for me. The culprits, they'd determined, were three recent college grads who truly didn't realize the seriousness of what they were doing. Their managers had investigated and confronted the young men, who were very contrite. It was clear that, by almost any standard, these were not bigots or hate mongers but good kids who'd made a horrible mistake for the sake of a laugh, without thinking about the implications, the consequences of their actions. By now, the entire New York office was aware of the situation. This was no longer a private matter. So what should we do? The question was ultimately in my lap as the CEO.

I faced a painful choice. However, as is so often the case, I didn't have complete freedom to respond however I saw fit. There were precedents and procedures I had to consider. Years before, Y&R had announced a policy of zero tolerance for sexual harassment and discrimination based on religion, race, or gender. The consequences for any violation of this policy were clearly spelled out: it would lead to dismissal. Every year, we'd sent around memos reinforcing the same policy. Every new employee was exposed to a video describing the company's ethical conduct mandates in detail.

This case involved youngsters who perhaps didn't fully deserve to be fired. It would have been easy to scold them, punish them, and give them a chance to redeem themselves. I wished badly to be able to do something like that. But was their behavior explainable to vast numbers of African American people in our company and elsewhere in our industry? Could it be tolerated and leave our anti-harassment policy intact? If no clear, decisive action was taken, how serious would our policy appear? It boiled down to a humanly difficult choice: Should we give these young people a second chance, or insist on following both the spirit and the letter of the policy?

To bend our own rule might have seemed compassionate to the violators, but not to those vulnerable to the racist implications of what they'd done. It would have violated our zero tolerance policy. So, sadly, we had to fire them. I still think about that decision—not questioning its correctness, but thinking about the impact on the three young men—and whenever I do, I hope they learned something profound and powerful from the experience. I wish them well.

It isn't always easy to make the clear and simple decisions. When consequences are minimal, it's easy enough to appear wise and just. But the impact on oneself and one's organization is greatest when the decisions are tough, when the answers aren't totally clear, and when the consequences are significant—and that's when sticking to values is not only most important but also most difficult.

The Missed Opportunity

The ability to make these decisions, to choose the right thing, in situations when the wrong thing seems the only guaranteed way to survive, can be harrowing. It comes, on its own, only through incessant practice. It's like an athletic skill, a golf swing. You have to make the right decisions at the small, seemingly minor crossroads, when big things aren't at stake, in order to choose the right direction when your path brings you to the edge of a precipice. I learned the hard way about the pain of dishonesty, and about how the only protection against making the wrong decisions is mindfulness, a watchfulness over myself, that extended even beyond my choices—a habit of looking back and being honest about the things I've chosen, after the fact. It was only through this practice of looking back and mulling over everything I'm doing that I was able to learn how to avoid, in advance, the kind of wrong choice I made with one dear friend, a choice I regret even now.

I met Ken Chenault more than fifteen years ago when I was president of Y&R International. Even then, he was a senior executive at American Express, and Y&R was one of several agencies working with him. We collaborated on many strategic initiatives, including the launch of the Optima card and a continuous series of repositionings of the AmEx brand, all designed to make it more relevant to consumers in the 1990s. Today, of course, Ken is the CEO of American Express, probably one of the most prestigious and powerful corporate posts held by any African American.

Throughout our relationship, I've watched with admiration as Ken strove constantly in true "Japanese" fashion for continuous improvement of the AmEx line of products and services. I've never met an executive so committed to his task, or one who put more into his job while exhibiting both creativity and ethics at an extraordinarily high level. What differentiates Ken in my mind is his passionate commitment to people, to the culture of the organization, and to helping support the many less-fortunate throughout our communities. In many ways, Ken is an extraordinary model of my definition of business success—great competence blended with honesty, respect, and accountability.

Barbara and I were also fortunate to get to know Ken and his wife, Kathy, as a couple and as parents. We visited them at their home in New Rochelle, and the closeness of the relationship between Kathy and Ken is heart-warming. Kathy herself was a very successful lawyer who decided to become a mother and also does an enormous amount of volunteer work on behalf of New York City and other communities.

The particular incident I'm about to relate dates back to 1997, a time when Y&R was working on AmEx's database marketing, which involved direct mail and direct TV. Our involvement with AmEx was not at the core of AmEx's business, and they brought us in to round out the excellent work Ogilvy & Mather was doing as their agency of record. Shelley Lazarus, the brilliant CEO of Ogilvy, had grown up on the AmEx account and continues to be one of the superstars of the industry. Ken was a very loyal person who would never needlessly abandon a partner. Given all these facts, I knew it was unlikely that Y&R would play a larger role with AmEx in the foreseeable future.

Out of the blue, Citibank contacted us about a major assignment—a U.S. brand campaign—that was significantly larger than our AmEx work. They wanted Y&R to participate in a competition for the business, but I declined, citing our relationship with AmEx. In my view, it would have been a conflict of interest to work on both accounts simultaneously. Citibank went ahead without us. But six or seven months later—they still hadn't picked an agency— they came back to us and upped the ante. What if Y&R got not just this project but the entire Citibank account on a global basis, and with no competition, provided Y&R could assure Citibank of the right level of staffing and agency commitment? It was impossible to ignore this opportunity.

Bill Campbell headed up consumer banking there, and he was a former client of ours. He knew Y&R and had the highest regard for Y&R and John McGarry, my partner and our president, in particular. Bill was a strong marketing person, who reported directly to Citibank's CEO, John Reed. The business decision for Y&R was fairly clear-cut. If we had been a core agency of AmEx, we would never have considered the switch, but AmEx represented only a fraction of the business Citibank could bring our way, and we weren't the AmEx agency of record. In its history, Y&R has to my knowledge never resigned a core client to get a larger or better one.

But this was different, and—from a purely business perspective—it was a slam-dunk decision.

But personally, it chafed. I found it impossible to tell Ken Chenault what we were going to do until it was upon us. While Y&R was negotiating terms with Citibank, it was important to maintain general secrecy. If the news were to leak, we all believed it might torpedo the deal. This is how I justified keeping the news to myself until the last minute. I knew, on a purely ethical basis—and as a natural consequence of our long friendship—Ken deserved some discreet advance notice. I agonized over this—literally had sleepless nights tossing around alternatives. I wasn't worried about Ken's reaction toward me, about what he might do if I told him. I always knew that outwardly he'd smooth it over and brush it off. He would even understand and agree with the business decision. But I also knew he'd be deeply hurt, and I didn't want that. Possibly, some part of me thought we might not win the Citibank account, and I could go on without ever telling him what we'd done.

Still I kept quiet, stalling, avoiding the issue. I rationalized day after day. If I burdened Ken with confidential information that he couldn't discuss with his colleagues, wouldn't I put him in an awkward position? He might have to sit on the news for a week or a few weeks. Perhaps he would consider it unfair, if I opened up with him about what was happening. That's how far afield I was able to go to deceive myself to justify my silence. Finally, the details of the deal were in place, at which point Citibank asked us not to inform AmEx until the morning of the public announcement.

I couldn't stand it any longer. I told Citibank I had to break the news to Ken at least one day in advance. So, only a day before we made the deal public, a colleague and I joined Ken for an awkward breakfast at his office. Of course, as I'd expected, Ken's reaction was very professional, polite, and businesslike. But after that day, there was a strain in our friendship, and it was immediately obvious to me how much I'd hurt him. I'd taken the self-protective approach—and the approach that implied I didn't trust Ken enough to confide in him about something that would have a significant impact on his business life. I had violated my fundamental rule about trust—Ken had never given me a reason not to trust him, and I should have told him everything in advance. But I didn't.

I ended up putting him in the awkward position of having to tell everyone else at AmEx the bad news only a day ahead, giving them no time to look for another agency to pick up the work once they lost us. I'd convinced myself that I was doing Ken a favor by waiting. Of course, Ken never complained, and to this day we've never fully discussed the incident. We've seen each other many times since then. But once you've done something, it can't be undone. I consider my behavior toward Ken a real lesson in how hard it can be to face the nature of what you do when you may have much to lose by sticking to your deepest beliefs. And my ability to look back on that incident with honesty has helped show me why, next time around—if and when a similar situation arises—I need to have the courage and will to make the right decisions. In the years afterward, when, at times, even larger things were at stake, and the easier, less honest path seemed even more tempting, the lesson I learned from Ken Chenault helped me do the right thing.

The Lost Glasses

Sometimes doing the right thing requires you to leave money on the table. It isn't a matter of risking short-term gain, but of turning it down, turning away work you'd gladly profit from under different circumstances. In the early 1980s, Warner-Lambert came to Y&R's new product development group looking for help in launching a new business. This great pharmaceutical company was considering a bold move into a new market. It wanted to create a line of Arthur Ashe sunglasses. Since many of Warner-Lambert's toiletries, confectionary, and proprietary drug products—Listerine, Halls, Dentyne, Rolaids,

Benadryl, and others—are sold in drugstores, often in close proximity to racks of sunglasses, this seemed like a fit, at least from a
merchandising perspective.

Warner-Lambert wasn't a Y&R client at the time, so we considered this an important prospect. It was a plum account: to be there
at the launch of a new, glamorous product line with the potential for
hip, fresh advertising. The team would have loved sunglasses: there
was great potential for cutting-edge work. It was all about style.
Almost any kind of work could have bolstered the core business
strategy of selling sunglasses. So, in this case, the strategy wouldn't
do much to dampen the thrill, as it often did. Anyone who has ever
created cookie-cutter advertising within the constraints of tight
graphic standards—size of typeface, relation of art to copy, and so
on—knows what a luxury it can be to have carte blanche with a
product that begs for out-of-the-box advertising. So it was the sort
of fun that a crew of writers and artists will kill to get, and it was also
an account that could offer us major revenue down the road.

There would definitely be some big money spent on the eyewear products, getting the line launched. Whether or not they
could grab market share from the likes of Ray-Ban and Oakley was
uncertain, but they would be spending millions to find out, and we
could ride that momentum toward high-profile advertising and
short-term profit. And, on top of everything else, our strength as a
full-service marketing solutions shop was just what they needed.
There was, in short, nothing unpleasant about the prospect of working for Warner-Lambert. It looked good from all angles—good fun
and good business. It could even help us make inroads into the
pharmaceutical business as a whole.

So, at the start, we were dying to impress them. We wanted that
account in the worst way. Yet our honesty began to eat away at our
passion. The longer we studied the economics of the sunglasses
business and the nature of the competition—Warner-Lambert's
positioning in relation to drugstores and other eyewear outlets, and

other factors—the more convinced we became that going into that market would be a costly failure. It was the old notion of sticking to your knitting: let your work stay close to your core competency and reap the rewards. Sunglasses weren't anywhere near Warner-Lambert's core business, except in their proximity to Dentyne gum on a drugstore's checkout counter shelves. This wasn't the message Warner-Lambert wanted to hear, nor was it one we especially wanted to deliver. But deliver it we did.

My good friend Craig Middleton and the Y&R team worked hard to create a proposal on why we *shouldn't* take the account—and why the company *shouldn't* sell shades. A few people, to say the least, considered this effort a bit counterproductive. It was a proposal designed to self-destruct sixty seconds after it was delivered. It certainly wasn't going to win us the eyewear business, but it was the truth. We decided to tell the client exactly what we thought. We were the only agency to take this stance.

We put our regrets about Warner-Lambert behind us. We moved on. In the end, Y&R's integrity—our ability to obey the principles of alignment and say no to some short-term revenue at the expense of the client's best interest—was rewarded. To our surprise, they came back and told us they agreed with our analysis and would back away from the business. Shortly thereafter, they hired us as an agency for other Warner-Lambert products. It was a terrific, profitable partnership that lasted over a dozen years. But even if we'd never heard from them again, it wouldn't change my view of what we did: it was the right thing, and the smart thing. The best way to build trust is to speak the truth when it offers you no short-term gain whatsoever. Honesty that brings no financial rewards—or even diminishes them—is *real* honesty.

The Moment of Truth

In 1982, Johnson & Johnson was a client of Young & Rubicam, so I found myself in the privileged position of seeing a classic business story unfold, from the inside, when Johnson & Johnson recalled more than 250,000 bottles of Tylenol after seven Chicagoans were killed by cyanide-laced capsules of the pain reliever. Jim Burke, then CEO of Johnson & Johnson, the makers of Tylenol, found himself in a situation where he and his company had everything to lose by being open about the facts—and he chose to be guided by honesty and trust. The Tylenol poisonings case is one of the best known, most dramatic, and most revealing case histories of how to do things the right way when everything seems to be falling apart—when fear is at its most extreme.

At the time, Burke had been CEO for six years. So he bore the responsibility of shepherding the brand, and the company, through one of the most profound crises in corporate history. For several weeks, Burke and his team had to manage amid an atmosphere of near-hysteria. Millions of Americans were terrified not only of taking Tylenol but of other pain remedies, fearing that a madman intent on random killing was at large. Rumors abounded, and any death that occurred in proximity to a Tylenol capsule set off alarms. Separating fact from fiction was remarkably difficult. One truck driver was found dead alongside the road with an opened Tylenol bottle nearby. His body tested positive for cyanide. It took a while for doctors to realize that the driver was a heavy smoker, and that smokers' bodies are often "cyanotic." He'd died of a heart attack—the presence of Tylenol was a mere coincidence. Under the circumstances, many observers doubted that the faith of the public in Tylenol, and perhaps in any over-the-counter medication, could ever be restored.

Burke and his team at Johnson & Johnson proved them wrong.

First, they responded with total candor, openness, and willingness to tell the truth, beginning with the very first reports of poisonings. It helped that they had nothing to hide, but Jim believed the public had the right to know everything the company knew. Second—and this was the toughest part—they made every decision with one overriding goal in mind: public safety. For example, both FBI Director William Webster and Arthur Hayes, head of the

FDA, urged J&J not to withdraw Tylenol from the market, fearing a national panic and worried that it might encourage copycat attacks. But Jim considered the risk of more poisonings simply too great.

It must have been immensely tempting to do what they'd suggested—to take the easy route and save large sums of money. If someone else were poisoned, Burke could point the finger at the federal government. But he insisted on pulling the product from the shelves. It was, he realized, the only way to completely guarantee the safety of those who used Tylenol.

J&J spent over $100 million recalling, testing, and destroying millions of bottles of capsules, and then spent millions more on replacing the capsules with less tamper-prone tablets. Then the company took the lead in developing new standards and procedures for making tamper-resistant packaging for over-the-counter medications, which the FDA quickly adopted. These were decisions with large short-term costs—and gigantic long-term benefits. Defying the odds, Tylenol regained 85 percent of its prior market share within a year and soon regained its position as the country's leading analgesic. Before long, sales were greater than ever.

Contrast the Tylenol story to the Firestone tire episode, in which deaths attributed to faulty tires have brought a great company to the brink of financial disaster. From the start, Firestone responded to the reports with a defensive stance—denying its own responsibility. There was no problem with the tires, only a problem with the design of the cars using them. That statement sums up the moral and professional failure—the lack of willingness to take responsibility. Trying to pin the blame on someone else was wrong. It was bad business, in every sense of the term, to conceal the data for years without bringing it to Ford and to the public. Firestone had made the tires, it had the data.

Firestone lost sight of the enormous difference between legal culpability—what you can get away with—and moral responsibility.

In that gray area thrives most of the bad faith that eventually brings a company down. Being able to get away with something doesn't make it good business. When Firestone celebrated its hundredth anniversary in 2000, who was going to light a firecracker? It's a tragic failure of stewardship and the corruption of a brand name that took a century to build. What the company lacked were the fundamental cornerstones: honesty and trust and a willingness to take a short-term hit, financially, out of concern for customer safety. That action denied alignment and denied customer focus.

By contrast, Burke and the J&J team were well aware of their responsibility to conserve the heritage of trust and integrity J&J had spent a hundred years building. From the moment the Tylenol crisis exploded, they were focused on that legacy of trust and everything was directed toward the welfare of millions of their customers, as well as the confidence health care professionals had placed in J&J products for decades.

Here is the where the truth of this episode becomes difficult to translate into simple instructional terms. Jim Burke's leadership arose directly from his character, not just from the practice of particular business skills. And character cannot be reduced to an abstraction—something that can be acquired from a book. It is forged through suffering, practice, restraint, and self-sacrifice. The way in which Jim's life transformed his character eventually enabled him to make some of the toughest choices any executive, any leader, ever has to make.

I asked Jim why he'd been able to choose to do the right thing, and he went back to his childhood, his formative years—and the strength that grew out of his own failures and weaknesses, his own personal pain. He told me he wasn't a precocious youngster marked for leadership from an early age. Just the opposite. He was a slow learner, often called immature. His body grew faster than his emotions and personality.

"It took me a long time to grow up emotionally," Jim says. "In fact, I was scared to death half the time."

Jim had to struggle for many years to achieve maturity. In many cases, when people are marked somehow with characteristics that single them out from the herd, the struggle to mature ultimately fails. They never grow up. Sometimes, they end up in prison, in mental institutions, or simply living half-lives of underachievement and failed relationships. But for others, the struggle for self-acceptance forges character. Jim agrees that, for him, the need to accept himself was something that he had to battle with over a period of years, into his adulthood.

"It was hard for me to face my own weaknesses and needs. But once I was able to do that, I became willing to reach out to a force of goodness in the universe that can give us strength and lift us above our personal failings. Call it God if you like, though I'm not religious in any conventional sense. But it's something greater than self that we can call upon when we need it—if we're willing to admit we need it," he said.

Burke drew strength, not despair, from the turmoil that surrounded him as a child and adolescent. His father had a clear, rigid sense of right and wrong. His mother was more intellectually curious and liked to challenge assumptions.

In family debates around the dinner table, Jim began to learn to reason, to argue, to struggle toward the truth. All four Burke children went on to have fascinating, often tumultuous lives and careers. Jim's best-known sibling is his brother Dan, who, with partner Tom Murphy, was one of the most influential and revered television network leaders ever at ABC, and the industry in general, during the 1980s. So an early experience of adversity, and growing up in a family where he was continually challenged both intellectually and emotionally, was an essential part of the background that prepared Jim for the crisis. The risk taking inherent in his decision to do the most ethical thing wasn't, in itself, a deterrent. He'd loved taking risks his entire life—it was, in fact, a problem for him.

"I used to be a compulsive gambler," he said. "There's probably not a casino in the country I haven't seen the inside of."

Risk taking was, in a way, an essential part of his life. Early in his career, Jim left Procter & Gamble after three and a half years, to join J&J. It was the first big stretch for him, and it pushed him to the limit of his abilities, testing his skills. Ultimately, he felt constrained, and he quit the corporate life to try his hand at entrepreneurship, launching three separate businesses, all of which failed. When he returned to J&J, he took on the new products division—which led to even more adversity. His first few years after his return were a sequence of failures. The company head, Robert Johnson II, known as The General because of his work running the New York Ordinance District during World War II, called Jim into his office. Jim expected to be fired. Instead, The General congratulated him for the fact that he kept finding new ways to fail.

"Don't ever make these mistakes again. But please make many other mistakes. That's what we're paying you for."

It was a remarkable and unforgettable lesson. It reinforced Jim's belief in himself and his certainty that, if he kept trying long enough, he'd win. It also gave him the sense that J&J was a safe place for experimentation, growth, and risk taking—a place that respected hard work and talent, even through times when it wasn't generating instant results. Those failures taught him fortitude, the refusal to be defeated—and were key to his courage during the Tylenol crisis. He'd seen the worst. He'd been there. He knew he could lead a company through terrible times without compromising his principles.

◆

The formative test of Jim's leadership arrived in a challenge to his company's mission statement. He discovered that the heart of his role was to make sure the company's operation reflected its core values. A labor leader at J&J approached him and said, "The Credo is bullshit." He was referring to the J&J Credo, a document created by The General in the 1940s. Though thirty years old, it was still one of the most admired corporate mission statements ever written: the vision and values of an entire company distilled into a simple statement Jim had never questioned. It's brief enough to quote in full:

> We believe our first responsibility is to the doctors, nurses and patients, to mothers and fathers and all others who use our products and services. In meeting their needs, everything we do must be of high quality. We must constantly strive to reduce our costs in order to maintain reasonable prices. Customers' orders must be serviced promptly and accurately. Our suppliers and distributors must have an opportunity to make a fair profit.
>
> We are responsible to our employees, the men and women who work with us throughout the world. Everyone must be considered as an individual. We must respect their dignity and recognize their merit. They must have a sense of security in their jobs. Compensation must be fair and adequate, and working conditions clean, orderly and safe. We must be mindful of ways to help our customers fulfill their family responsibilities. Employees must feel free to make suggestions and complaints. There must be equal opportunity for employment, development and advancement for those qualified. We must provide competent management, and their actions must be just and ethical. We are responsible to the communities in which we live and work and to the world community as well. We must be good citizens—support good works and charities and bear our fair share of taxes. We must encourage civic improvement and

better health and education. We must maintain in good order the property we are privileged to use, protecting the environment and natural resources.

Our final responsibility is to our stockholders. Business must make a sound profit. We must experiment with new ideas. Research must be carried on, innovative programs developed, and mistakes paid for. New equipment must be purchased, new facilities provided, and new products launched. Reserves must be created to provide for adverse times. When we operate according to these principles, the stockholders should realize a fair return.

Jim had long been a believer in the Credo, so the labor leader's words were one of the toughest challenges he'd ever faced. "The shock of hearing him say that changed me more than anything else I went through at J&J. It shook all my assumptions about the company. I realized the company's value system had drifted away from it."

When he became president of J&J, those words were still ringing in his ears: *The Credo is bullshit.* Jim set out to make sure no one ever had a reason to repeat them. He set up the now-famous Credo Challenge meetings to explore the J&J mission and how the company could make it real. This, too, was a kind of risk taking (especially when Burke arranged to have the sessions filmed), because these meetings could easily unravel into exercises in cynicism or complaint. But Jim had enough faith in the strength of the Credo and the integrity of J&J's people that he was willing to take those risks. The result was a series of frank, intense conversations among a wide range of J&J executives, arguing out the implications of the Credo and battling over its relevance to contemporary business.

Jim Burke likens these sessions to the arguments around his family's dinner table—crucibles out of which a closer approximation to truth might emerge. This event turned out to be crucial in preparing J&J—and Jim Burke—for the Tylenol poisonings six years later.

"These sessions helped us solidify our values," he now says. "The Credo was reworded, modernized, and reaffirmed. By the time the crisis came, I trusted the culture, and the people who worked within it."

The Credo became, once again, the heart of how the company operated. Still, when the crisis hit, it took him almost two weeks to grasp what was at stake and to understand what he had to do. He told me he was deeply frightened about what might happen. He pulled together a team of eight people, who met around a conference table day and night, hammering out plans of action.

But, in the end, the choices made around that conference table saved the Tylenol brand and perhaps J&J as well. The company took a hit. Its stock dropped dramatically. Soon enough, it rose to new heights. By focusing first on their responsibility to consumers and the general public, Burke and his team ultimately positioned their company for enormous financial benefits. (In a recent Harris survey, J&J was ranked as having the most sterling reputation of any corporation in the world.) If they'd pursued the opposite tack, seeking to deny responsibility, to defend the company, and to protect short-term profits, they might well have lost everything. Y&R played a supporting role in the crisis, helping Jim Burke and his colleagues through the most challenging moments, and we were able to do that only because we believed in the Credo as much as Jim did.

In their moments of crisis, leaders respond in their own ways. When Enron was about to implode, Chairman Ken Lay, with a straight face, told the outside world and his nervous employees that everything was fine and a new era of prosperity for Enron was about to unfold. At the same time, he quickly sold millions of dollars of Enron stock while the getting out was still good. But when Jim Burke faced the greatest crisis of his career, he acted from the foundation of his character and did the right thing, regardless of the risk. And his company, eventually, was rewarded handsomely for years to come.

Values are no longer a luxury in business. They are no longer optional codes of behavior just for the good guys. Values are the essential principles that guide a company's or a brand's vision and make the behavior of competent, motivated employees fit an organization's core mission. Consistent application of core values is the critical facilitator for proper alignment among all critical company constituencies.

If you want a consistently successful business life and a fulfilled personal life, you must dare to be good. Good at all the five enduring business principles, but especially good at values. If you dare to be good at the thousands of small decisions, you will do the big ones right when it comes time to put your integrity to the test. You will be a great businessperson by being a good human being.

There is a wonderful addendum to Jim Burke's life story. After he retired from J&J, he started the most worthy "Partnership for Drug Free America," which uses volunteer advertising agencies, media, and some government investment to convince America's youngsters not to take drugs. The effort has had a significant positive impact in the long struggle to diminish drug usage. For his character, for his values, for winning his own personal struggle for good, for his real achievements in the face of adversity, Jim was honored by Congress and the president with the Medal of Freedom, the highest nonmilitary recognition our country can bestow on one of its citizens.

POSTSCRIPT

A Better Chance

The twenty-first-century environment will be challenging at every level: for America as a nation, for the world at large, for achieving and sustaining peace. A lot of smart people will have to do the right, courageous things for our children and grandchildren to have the lives adult Americans have enjoyed since the Second World War. In this environment, business success will come with ever greater need for industry and wisdom. Simple hard work and effort, while essential, just won't get you there. Products and services, through brands, will have to continually differentiate themselves, while maintaining relevance and building ever-stronger bonds with their respective customers. It all depends on continual innovation. It is critical for us in this nation to adapt creativity as our number one business priority, as the most critical business strategy to ensure our continued prosperity and growth.

Productive creativity in business doesn't happen spontaneously, does not rise up out of a vacuum. It requires hard work by well-trained, committed men and women. Enduring competencies, as well as the new ones, will be essential to leverage their creative energies. We will need enlightened leaders who understand the necessity for all this and the critical value of productive employees who can set the right vision and mission for the company, and who introduce the right values as the compass of behavior to meet those company objectives. In this spirit, we have to debunk the sports analogy, where there can only be winners and losers. This kind of polarity doesn't hold for business. While the competitive spirit in business will forever be essential for motivation, business can have many winners. For the twenty-first-century organization, sustainable success and profitability will come as by-products of correct vision and brilliant execution.

The five principles discussed in this book will guarantee this sustainable achievement: creativity, competence, enlightened leadership, alignment, and values. Practicing these five principles with consistency over time is the new source of success. They are all totally intertwined. To adopt these principles requires rigor, discipline, and a lifetime of continuous learning. These are not techniques of the day. They will illuminate the path to success and personal fulfillment for generations. They require the same kind of hard work and dedication needed to master a craft, perfect an athletic skill, or hone an individual creative style in the arts. But you can't pick and choose among these five areas. Whether you are a CEO or a new brand manager, you must practice and perfect your skills in all five areas until they become second nature.

We can learn and become very proficient in all these essential principles. Again, through dedication, hard work, and practice, we can become successful and personally fulfilled. That's as close to a guarantee as an honest person can give. But in the spirit of openness and honesty, this entire book is premised on the assumption that a human being has the capacity to change in a radical way in order to succeed in life. To be a good businessperson, you must in fact be a good person. Can we, as human beings, reinvent ourselves through the resolve and capacity to change for the better? Can we live by the ground rules of enlightened leadership? Can we practice creativity, alignment, the demanding values of honesty, trust, integrity, respect for others and ourselves, and accountability? This book assumes we can and will.

In many ways, the discipline required to live by these principles goes against defensive instincts wired deeply into our being. Even in good times, these imperatives can chafe. Under pressure, in a crisis, our survival instincts simmer up: we're hardwired to revert to leadership that inspires fear. To uncover a new foundation for our own behavior—to build it on principles that express what makes us most human until it becomes as natural and familiar as breathing—can require enormous practice and effort over an extended period of time. Seen especially in the stories of Jim Burke and Bill George, it can require a lifetime of commitment and self-training and a persistent willingness to question one's own behavior. To someone mired in the old ways of getting the job done, it might seem like nothing less than an attempt to reengineer human nature. As daunting as it may sound, there's a joy that emerges from the effort—an appetite for it—the sense that you are becoming the person you *want* to be, not the person you have to be, and your organization feels that and follows.

It can be done, and it gets easier as you go.

As I mentioned at the start of Chapter Six, early in my career I went through something of a spiritual crisis. Through relaxation techniques and meditation, I began to connect with an inner energy that, I felt, would help guide me toward what was good. So my goal became to draw from this energy in a sustainable way, by becoming as free as possible from my own destructive instincts. I came to this view of myself, and the practice of meditation, in part, through my reading of Paul Ehrlich. Ehrlich, an evolutionary biologist at Stanford, wrote books about human nature itself, and how genetics govern much of human behavior.

Through these other writings, I discovered theories that helped me understand how much of what we call "evil" in human behavior is a way of acting out survival instincts. In *New World, New Mind*, Ehrlich lays out his theory that most behavior we call evil originates in primitive reflexes built into the human organism as it evolved out of the jungle. In other words, what we consider evil now once kept us all alive: it wasn't evil, back then. It was absolutely *necessary*. It sustained the human race. But we've outgrown it, and the behavior that once kept us alive now threatens us.

Intellectually, Ehrlich's theories did for me what meditation did behaviorally: they gave me an anchor, a foundation, upon which to rebuild the way I did things around a new ethical understanding. My reading of Ehrlich deepened as I grew older, and my ongoing passion for Ehrlich's ideas was strengthened through a visit I made to Poland, during which I toured the sites of the World War II concentration camps at Auschwitz. The unspeakable reality of these camps had a profound effect on me. It ignited an intense, inward questioning about the purpose of human life. How could this possibly happen? How could we do this to one another? I was, in a sense, captured by this question. It wouldn't let go of me. It became, more than ever before, a central preoccupation.

Ehrlich's theories offered a way of, if not reconciling myself to such evil, at least coping with it. He hypothesized that people commit evil mostly when they are responding to a perceived threat. They project it onto others and then seek to destroy or disarm the other as a way of feeling more secure, more powerful, or more alive. In the jungle, life was largely a matter of defeating or destroying an enemy, first animal predators and then human ones. We've left the jungle behind, but we've brought our instincts, built into our DNA, into the present moment—through defensive behavior built into the human organism—and these instincts are woven deeply into the fabric of business. The impulses don't simply go away because you wear a suit and live in a penthouse—it's become a commonplace assumption, in some circles, that they *enable* you to do those things.

Whatever one thinks of Ehrlich's theories, they offered me a way to stand back, looking at my own responses to what I saw as threats to my success, and manage not just the threats (by understanding them) but my own reaction to them. I realized my central challenge wasn't something outside in the world; it was within myself. I began to become responsible for my response to things I couldn't control, as well as for the outcome of things I could influence. In effect, it gave me a way of choosing to do good—restraining myself from my own worst impulses, and at least understanding them in a way that helped me work around them more effectively.

A new model emerged for me, a new way of working with other people, of doing business, and of being myself, based on this recognition of the human inclination for evil in the most ordinary circumstances. Human nature can be improved, or at least tempered, through conscious choices, through disciplines like meditation and prayer—or simply a fierce, relentless self-awareness, a willingness to listen and see things about yourself that you don't want to know. People can learn to free themselves from blind passions, as well as from the fight-or-flight reflexes of the jungle.

Is it really necessary to change? Ehrlich says yes. He theorizes that the world has reached a turning point, an evolutionary emergency: a time when human beings must speed up the process of cultural evolution through conscious choice. Survival-oriented fight-or-flight behavior that once ensured the continuance of the human race will now do just the opposite. Nuclear weapons, other weapons of mass destruction, the steady erosion of the ecological balance, global warming—all these represent a crisis demanding fundamental changes in human behavior, from confrontation to cooperation, from exploitation to respect, from wasteful consumption of our planet to conserving the fragile ecosystem. And then, of course, such shifts will demand a fundamentally new way to behave in business. To allow the creative act to flourish, to nurture and support our colleagues, to learn to be tough and demanding without being mean, while always being fair—it means practicing business in a new way that capitalizes on the genius of free enterprise and the customer-centric realities of an excess supply world.

To achieve this requires a new kind of *conscious evolution*. This is quite a leap, and, admittedly, it's a rather bold proposal for a book about success in the business world. Is human nature really able to alter itself this way, through conscious choice? Can leaders in business really free themselves from the destructive patterns that have served so well down through history—until now? Can we turn on a dime this way and go in a new direction?

Together, we can. It can't be done alone. We all need help. None of us stands on our own. We may be self-starters, but we aren't self-finishers. This book defines the context for business success over the next twenty or thirty years, and it offers a strategy for succeeding in that world, and finally it suggests that people who have the will to change *can* change. At the start of this book, I included an epigraph: "Many have the will to win. Few have the will to prepare." Implicit behind these words is this: you can have the will, you can learn the way—and you must have both—but neither is entirely sufficient. Even when you have both, it is often not sufficient. You can seldom succeed alone. Life is about teamwork, and teamwork is about the essential need for help from others.

As I learned in my liberation from Romania, and again and again as I found myself with a new life in America, there is no such thing as the self-made man or woman. The "I" is an illusion. The "we" is the only reality. My experiences in coming to this country, the breaks I got from compassionate and insightful people all along the way, are proof of this. Leading is simply the highest and most powerful way of serving something more important than yourself. I could cite dozens of lives, social programs, and corporate initiatives—a wealth of evidence showing that people can change in astonishing ways if they are given a chance, and if they have hope in their own ability to help change the world around them.

But I'm going to offer one example as proof that conscious evolution is possible, that human beings have nearly limitless potential to undergo radical changes and overcome enormous obstacles—with a little help from their friends.

It's a New York–based program called A Better Chance, and for three decades it has found and supported more than eleven thousand young people of color from the inner cities of America, giving them an opportunity for the highest-quality education possible—with almost invariably successful outcomes. It identifies students from underprivileged backgrounds who usually test in the lowest tenth of the population and offers them an opportunity to catch up. It offers these children access to some of the nation's most academically rigorous college prep programs in public schools and private boarding schools. Its college preparatory program includes 250 member schools offering A Better Chance students more than $20 million in full and partial scholarships through their associated secondary schools. It's a nonprofit organization that has an incredible record for turning bright minority kids into high achievers and community leaders by helping them win admission into great colleges and universities.

One-third of these students come from homes at or below the poverty level. Most come from low-income and working-class families. Two-thirds of these students are African American, a quarter Hispanic, 7 percent Asian, and 2 percent Native American. Graduates of A Better Chance include Tracy Chapman, singer and songwriter; Bernard Beal, a Wall Street financier managing billions; William Lewis Jr., now a partner at Lazard Freres & Co.; Deval Patrick, former U.S. assistant attorney general for civil rights and former general counsel for Coca-Cola. A Better Chance is one of the few 1960s-style Great Society programs to survive into this century. It was founded by twenty-three New England prep school headmasters who met at Phillips Academy in Andover, Massachusetts, to discuss how to help minority students. Part of the key to the program's success is identifying the most promising students, despite all evidence to the contrary: often these students have exceedingly low test scores. One applicant from Texarkana, Arkansas, scored in only the 21st percentile on the PSAT, yet he was recruited on other evidence of his potential, and went on to graduate from Milton Academy as a class valedictorian and recipient of two distinguished awards for academic excellence.

◆

Ed Young was one such youth. In kindergarten, he dreamed of being a schoolteacher and a principal. Growing up in Washington, D.C., he bribed his playmates with Oreo cookies and grape juice into being the pupils of the summer-long play-schools he held in his living room. Being a teacher or a principal might seem a modest goal. But for those growing up black in a tough, inner-city neighborhood, just getting through school seemed almost unattainable. Drugs, alcohol, gangs, violence, and despair claimed all too many.

Ed's future changed when his junior high school counselor, Mrs. Flowers, recommended Ed for participation in A Better Chance. With the help of A Better Chance, Ed was accepted in 1969 at Governor Dummer Academy in Bayfield, Massachusetts. He thrived. He acted in school plays, sang in the glee club, and edited the yearbook. Eventually, as a senior, he was awarded the Morris Flag, Governor Dummer's highest honor. He went on to graduate from Middlebury College, spent several years in Dallas as director of admissions and financial aid at St. Mark's School of Texas, and then returned to Governor Dummer Academy, where he was assistant headmaster and dean of admissions. In the spring of 2001, he was appointed head of All Saints Episcopal School in Phoenix, Arizona, the culmination of his childhood dream. It turns out Ed's goal was not in the least modest. Being a teacher and a principal, touching young lives, shaping futures is the noblest of professions.

Ed's story is typical of the children who have gone through A Better Chance, often born in the ghettos of New York, Los Angeles, Atlanta, and Chicago, and in many small towns of the Deep South. Overall, more than 90 percent of the Better Chance kids entering high school are graduated from college. That's a staggering statistic. A good many of these kids grow up in a snake pit. Often their parents are separated, too often with a father addicted, in prison, or gone much of the time. Their playgrounds are a jungle, and the drug economy is ever-present, offering escape and a doomed promise of opportunity. They are residents, essentially, of a Third World inside America's borders.

A tough-minded despair is the norm in these neighborhoods. I saw this firsthand in an unforgettable way, earlier in my career. At Young & Rubicam, in one of our pro bono initiatives to convince children under eighteen years old to stop smoking, we discovered how tough it would be. As always, we did research to discover the emotional hot buttons. I was there in Harlem, in a makeshift facility, watching through a two-way mirror, as I listened to a group of teens talk about smoking. In the midst of some banal conversation, one young man lashed out at the focus group moderator.

"I'm fifteen. I've got maybe two years to live in this place. Tell me why the hell I should stop smoking," he said.

I'll never forget the indisputable logic of his despair. He had no way out. He *could* stop smoking, but a bullet would kill him at a younger age and more efficiently than cancer, which would only be a threat if he was still around thirty years later. A Better Chance is one of the few programs that offer a real response to that hopelessness and that bullet. It promises these youths that they can become productive citizens and have a place in this society and this economy.

Since 1963, A Better Chance has been recruiting minorities, mostly from inner cities, kids who are bright, hard-working, and gifted, but lack one or more obvious markers by which talent is usually recognized and rewarded. It has four thousand volunteers in communities around the United States who find these special kids, and they help place them in some of the best secondary schools in America—independent day schools like Collegiate School, The Spence School, and the Athenian School; boarding schools like Philips Exeter Academy, Miss Porter's School, and Choate Rosemary Hall, and well-financed suburban public schools like New Trier, outside Chicago, Greenwich High, Wilton High, Wellesley High, and so many more. Many go on to become class presidents or valedictorians, and again, more than 90 percent of the graduates enter college immediately.

The people who have run A Better Chance are admirable, a shining example of the sort of leadership I've been talking about. Judith Griffin, who led the organization for nearly thirty years, is one such person. Her life became the well-being of these kids. She was passionately committed, living proof of goodness in a human being. Young Sandra Timmons, the organization's new leader, is an equally committed, determined, passionate worker supporting this organization's great cause.

Sandra has surrounded herself with many caring believers, supporters, and contributors. A good many are graduates of A Better Chance. Others are there because they have seen how the program makes a difference. Because A Better Chance is about all these kids, the ghetto kids, our kids. And finally, there's Oprah Winfrey. She heard, she saw, she carefully looked into the seriousness of the organization. Her own personal life story of abuse and enormous struggle made her empathize with A Better Chance kids. She was, in spirit, one of them. By now, she's given more than $13 million to the program. Oprah's one of the great guardian angels and one very special, classy human being.

A goodly number of representatives of corporate America give to this program already, rather generously. These corporate leaders have discovered a simple equation. They have seen how this program—*based on the assumption that human beings can almost routinely transform themselves in a radical way*—harvests future leaders of our society. No other system—the existing school system, the job placement industry, the human resources capabilities of our industries—no other system locates and cultivates this sort of leadership, lifting people from the depths to the heights.

What's most significant about A Better Chance, in the context of this book, is that these students, more often than not, prove to be among the hardest workers, the most creative leaders, the wisest managers. They are, in effect, a smart bet, a smart investment, and a smart hire. This program offers an example of a way for private enterprise to rethink the fundamentals: especially some of our deepest assumptions about nature and nurture and what's possible for individual human beings, given the right circumstances, to achieve. It's premised on the assumption that anyone who hopes to lead must be a hero—and that nearly anyone can become such a hero, given the opportunity. And heroes, as Joseph Campbell once pointed out, are always the same thing, everywhere in the world: human beings who, by confronting the darkness within and around themselves and transforming themselves for the better, make it possible for others to do the same. Remarkable transformations are the essence of our deepest myths about human life, and we've seen how such transformations have been inherent in the leadership of the best CEOs. With only the slightest encouragement—the sort of encouragement that comes naturally to a workforce, for example, when a leader follows the principles of this book—human beings can become the same kind of leaders at all levels of life. The energy and good will it requires is innate in human nature. For thirty years, A Better Chance has been proving this faith in people.

◆

While A Better Chance may seem a bit of a detour in a book about principles for success in business, the program clearly illustrates an inherent human potential for change—of the deepest sort. Radical change isn't just possible, it's essential, and, in the end, quite natural. There's no greater joy than becoming the person you most deeply want to be, despite all the temptations to follow what might seem a more expedient path. Becoming that person, fulfilling your deepest potential, doesn't happen by forcing these changes. Commit to change, and you will change.

Everything in this book is already a natural human impulse—even though most of us have at some point learned to behave otherwise, because the world for so long has required it. Well, the world's requirements have changed in a revolutionary way—it *is* the end of the world as we've known it, and human nature can feel pretty fine in meeting this new world's demands. It may take will and determination and a certain endurance, at first, because not everyone around you will be heeding this call, but you will be uncovering your own your true nature, clearing away many of the behaviors that obscure what makes us all human. And there's a real joy in being able to do this.

If you're part of the world of business, the five enduring principles of this book are the key to this radical change. Behind all these principles is the assumption of fundamental personal change, not simply in your personality for work but in your deepest sense of yourself, the person you are in your whole life. To manage for creativity, you need to become less fearful about the future—less prone to force progress in your organization and more willing to inspire the kind of new, inventive approaches to growth that become essential to market differentiation. When you manage under pressure in tough times with trust and encouragement, in a culture that nurtures creative solutions, it requires a fundamental change in character, a willingness to live with the uncertainty that rides alongside trust and faith in your people. That kind of trust and faith inspires love and delight, not fear, even in the grip of the toughest challenges—and what follows is a new kind of trust in yourself, trust in your principles and values. The new competency of customer focus requires the same sort of change toward an outer-directed focus, a shift from selfish, internal organizational measures and preoccupations and toward a willingness to learn from customers and the market—a new kind of humility.

It isn't hard to see how that humility can spill over into all areas of your life. Enlightened leadership can take years, even decades, of practice, self-analysis, and an ever-renewed commitment to change—so that, when you are faced with the toughest ethical choices, you will make the right ones. Again, once you've gone through this crucible, it will influence everything you do, not just what you do at work. Alignment, which seems a purely organizational principle, is inherently ethical and requires a commitment to honesty in all walks of life. And all the values required of anyone who dares to be good—integrity, accountability, and all the others—are really the fruit of the changes in character implied by these basic principles. You can't run an organization by these values without being the same person with everyone, at work and at home.

It should be quite obvious by now that these changes will have a profound impact on you as a person. To become someone able to adapt to the demands of the excess supply economy—to be good in the terms of this book—is to be able to be the same person everywhere else. If you learn to be good at your work, if these principles become innate to the way you live, then you will be a better parent, a better spouse, a better friend. To have a fulfilled life, you will be good day and night, close to home and far away. The ultimate source of success is also the path toward personal happiness. And this can turn your career into something much more than simply a way to make a living—it can now be a way to make a life.

The journey ahead for you, no matter your age or state of career development, will be exciting and uplifting. Just follow the path, have confidence in yourself, and keep practicing. And, by the way, plan on enjoying it. Once you get the hang of it, you'll want the path to just keep on going. And it will.

Acknowledgments

In the modern era, the *I* word increasingly loses power to the *We*. Certainly that has been true in my case, all my life.

The book talks about the rich inheritance I received from my parents. It doesn't celebrate the extraordinary supportive faces that have helped me develop toward my potential.

At the top of the list is my wife and partner, Barbara. During our forty-year relationship so far, she has coached, prodded, provided air cover, done everything imaginable to enable me to grow and mature as a person and succeed as a professional.

I owe a great deal to the institution called Young & Rubicam. A brilliant company: creative, caring for its people, client-focused, consumer sensitive, innovative. The power of this company from its inception continues in the twenty-first century. I wish the next generations well.

The list of mentors and colleagues at Young & Rubicam who were part of my success is long and their contributions rich and selfless.

I was fortunate to learn from a number of outstanding client CEOs and managers whose friendship and support were consequential.

In the writing of this book, I am grateful to my partners: the brilliant writer Dave Dorsey and the wise editor-coach Dick Todd. Thanks also to my good friend and colleague, Ram Charan. Earlier in the long saga of this book's evolution, Peter Osnos and Karl Weber more than earned my appreciation. My keen publisher Susan Williams and her colleagues at Jossey-Bass who believed in this book also deserve my appreciation and gratitude.

Finally, I am inspired by my son Andrew's extraordinary human qualities and explosive talent as he begins to apply his values, competence, and creativity in following his dreams.

P.G.

The Authors

PETER A. GEORGESCU is chairman emeritus of Young & Rubicam (Y&R), a network of preeminent commercial communications companies dedicated to helping clients build their businesses through the power of brands. He served as the company's chairman and CEO from 1994 to 2000.

Georgescu was the first chairman of Y&R born outside the United States. His career spans thirty-seven years, both in the United States and Europe. He was instrumental in developing the integrated communications strategy that shaped the course of Y&R's development and became the standard for industry thinking. He has served as president of Y&R Advertising, as well as president of Y&R's former international division.

Under his leadership, Y&R successfully transformed from a private to a publicly held company. Also during his tenure, Y&R built the most extensive database on global branding and, from its findings, developed a proprietary model for diagnosing and managing brands. Within the marketing community, he is known as a leading proponent of creating unified communications programs, agency accountability for measuring the impact of communications programs, and structuring value-based agency compensation. In recognition of his contributions to the marketing and advertising industry, he was elected to the Advertising Hall of Fame in 2001.

Georgescu emigrated to the United States from Romania in 1954. He was educated at Exeter Academy, earning a B.A. cum laude from Princeton and an M.B.A. from the Stanford Business School. His belief in the power of education has fueled his involvement with organizations such as A Better Chance and Polytechnic University, both of which he serves as a member of the board of directors. The University of Alabama and Cornell College in Iowa have awarded him honorary doctorates. He is also the recipient of the Ellis Island Medal of Honor.

Georgescu serves as a board member of several publicly registered companies, including Levi's, International Flavors & Fragrances, EMI, and Toys "R" Us. He also serves as vice chairman of New York Presbyterian Hospital, as a trustee of A Better Chance, and is a member of the Council on Foreign Relations.

DAVID DORSEY is author of *The Force*, an account of a year in the life of a top salesman and his team at Xerox Corporation. Published by Random House in 1994 and in paperback by Ballantine in 1995, it was hailed by reviewers as "an uncompromising portrait of a modern salesman." It was picked as one of the ten best business books of the year by *BusinessWeek*, and the *New York Times* selected it as an Editor's Choice. His first novel, *The Cost of Living*, was published by Viking/Penguin in 1997. Since then he has been working on his second novel, *The Turning Season*, a love story, and is doing research for another nonfiction narrative on the lives of people in a small, rapidly growing telecommunications company.

Dorsey received his undergraduate degree in English and philosophy at the University of Rochester. He earned two master's degrees, one in English and one in communications, from the University of Illinois, where he taught a freshman literature course for two years. He worked as a reporter and editor for the *Great Falls Tribune* in Great Falls, Montana, in the late 1970s and early 1980s.

He was a reporter, editor, and editorial writer at the *Utica Observer-Dispatch* in the early 1980s. Later, he moved to Rochester to work as a business reporter and then business editor at the *Rochester Democrat & Chronicle*. In the late 1980s, he spent four years at Buck & Pulleyn, a marketing and communications agency, editing corporate magazines while writing freelance stories for *New England Monthly*. He has since been a freelance writer, contributing to *Fast Company, Esquire, Inc.*, and other magazines. He resides in Pittsford, New York, with his wife, Nancy. His son is a student at Newhouse School of Communications at Syracuse University and his daughter works for New Line Cinema in Los Angeles.

RAM CHARAN is a consultant to business leaders and best-selling coauthor of *Confroting Reality, Execution, The Discipline of Getting Things Done*, and *The Leadership Pipeline*.

Index